matthew mitcham

twists and turns

matthew mitcham

twists and turns

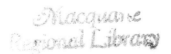 HarperCollins*Publishers*

HarperCollins*Publishers*

First published in Australia in 2012
by HarperCollins*Publishers* Australia Pty Limited
ABN 36 009 913 517
harpercollins.com.au

Copyright © Matthew Mitcham and Larry Writer 2012

Quote on page ix from *Toy Story*, Pixar 1995.

The right of Matthew Mitcham to be identified as the author
of this work has been asserted by him in accordance
with the *Copyright Amendment (Moral Rights) Act 2000*.

HarperCollins*Publishers*
Level 13, 201 Elizabeth Street, Sydney NSW 2000, Australia
31 View Road, Glenfield, Auckland 0627, New Zealand
A 53, Sector 57, Noida, UP, India
77–85 Fulham Palace Road, London W6 8JB, United Kingdom
2 Bloor Street East, 20th floor, Toronto, Ontario M4W 1A8, Canada
10 East 53rd Street, New York NY 10022, USA

ISBN 978 0 7322 9489 2 (pbk)
ISBN 978 1 7430 9508 9 (ebook)

Cover design by Darren Holt, HarperCollins Design Studio
Front image © John McRae 2012. Courtesy Ausin Tung Gallery, Melbourne
Back cover image by Terry Trewin. Courtesy Funky Trunks
Typeset in Sabon by Kirby Jones
Printed and bound in Australia by Griffin Press
The papers used by HarperCollins in the manufacture of this book
are a natural, recyclable product made from wood grown in sustainable
plantation forests. The fibre source and manufacturing processes meet
recognised international environmental standards, and carry certification.

5 4 3 2 1   12 13 14 15

To Marcus, Mia and Ky

contents

prologue   1

1   'no, sweetheart, you were not an accident'   5

2   my first true love   27

3   taking the plunge, and other diving puns   41

4   the black dog (matt's best friend)   63

5   retirement is for old folks   81

6   lifeline   109

7   back on the 'straight' and narrow   127

8   beijing bound   143

9   gold   155

10   fame games   177

11   up and up   193

12   beneath the surface   201

13   breaking point   219

14   body blow   231

15   london bound   251

16   olympic fever   257

17   all bets are off   271

18   growing up   295

Thank you …   303

Picture credits   305

About the author   307

Career highlights   309

'That's not flying.
That's just … falling with style!'

Woody, *Toy Story*

prologue

I stood in the stark concrete spiral staircase between the 7.5 metre and 10 metre towers waiting to take my turn. This was the only place during the competition where you were completely hidden from all people and cameras, where you didn't have to convey this to the judges or portray that to the cameras and crowds. The only place free from all external factors, leaving you alone with your mind — the powerful, unpredictable, influential entity that cultivates optimism and determination, or undermines confidence and sabotages outcomes. This is the place where you are most vulnerable to your mind's will.

As I took the last few steps up to the 10 metre platform, I gave myself no chance of winning gold. I had qualified for the finals of the 2008 Beijing Olympic Games, but as the 12 competitors lined up to perform our sixth and final dive, the dive that would decide the medallists, it seemed to me that it would take a series of extremely unlikely events to deprive hometown hero Zhou Luxin of the gold medal that would give China a clean sweep of every diving event at the Games.

If I was to claim the gold medal, something that no Australian man had done in diving since 1924, I would have to perform nothing less than the highest-scoring dive in Olympic history.

I fixed my hair, because I knew there would be millions of eyes watching me — I wanted to look good. Some of the other finalists appeared stressed, trudging disconsolately towards the stairs leading to the 10 metre tower as if a noose awaited them at the top. In contrast, I looked excited.

It was time. I stepped out onto the platform, and my mantra kicked in. 'Do your best, that's all you can do. Don't worry about the score. Relax … relax … enjoy this moment. Relax … enjoy it …' People who were there have told me that I didn't walk, I sauntered. My body felt powerful but light, as though I was dancing along the platform, weightless.

I stood a few metres back from the end of the platform, waiting for my name to boom out of the speakers and reverberate through the Water Cube. I continued repeating my relaxation mantra. I was in my zone. This was the place where all the drama, failures and triumphs of my life had brought me. This was where I needed to be.

I walked to the end of the platform, turned around and adjusted my foot position. All the background noise was completely drowned out by an uncanny silence. The infinite rows of spectators on either side of me faded to nothing. Time slowed down. I inhaled, exhaled and took off. I saw the lights in the ceiling and the bright blue water below, my body instinctively snapping into my most difficult dive, the back two and a half somersault with two and a half twists. My take-off was explosive, my movements fluid. Seconds later when I entered the water, neat and straight, I knew that I had done well. Maybe very well.

I stayed underwater for as long as my lungs would allow me, wondering if perhaps I had done well enough to exceed my every expectation and win an Olympic silver medal.

I surfaced to the sound of the crowd going bananas, and Mum and my boyfriend, Lachlan, were leaping out of their seats ... and my coach, Chava, was jumping up and down with his arms in the air, grinning from ear to ear. That's when I knew I had done it. Something incredible had happened.

Later, people would remark they were surprised that a gold medal and fame hadn't changed me. I always responded, 'Why would I change? Being me is the easiest person to be'.

I was lying. It wasn't.

1

'no, sweetheart, you were not an accident'

I was born in Brisbane's Queen Elizabeth II Hospital on March 2, 1988. Mum was two weeks late, then in labour with me for more than 24 hours. When I finally decided to emerge, I popped out, squawked a lot and marked my arrival into the world by weeing all over Mum and the doctors. Mum tells me that while she didn't take her contraceptive pill and one 'slipped past the goalie', I was no accident, more an 'unplanned surprise ... but a good one'.

My mum, Vivienne, and my father, Greg, broke up before I was born. She hadn't known my father too long, and they had only been seeing each other for a few months. Mum was just 18 and Greg 21, both still kids themselves, and he found the prospect of fatherhood, with all its responsibilities, just too scary.

Mum, of course, was front and centre in my life when I was small. Although she had boyfriends who stayed with us for periods, she raised me on her own, at houses in Brisbane's Carina and Camp Hill. The Carina place was where my grandparents, Marion and Harold Mitcham, lived before they split up and where they raised my mum, and Aunty Jo and Uncle Lenny. Our Camp Hill residence was not exactly a house but half a house. The bungalow was still owned by my grandad, who let one half of the house to us and the other to tenants, who came and went. For as long as I can remember, my grandparents have been apart. Grandma, who is a strong and intelligent woman in her 60s today, still lives alone in a typical Queenslander home in Tarana Street, Camp Hill.

I have inherited Mum's eyes and her naughtiness. She has been called difficult and a little self-absorbed, and so have I. She was, and still is, a proud and feisty woman – some might say *too* feisty. My mum is a unique, zesty, larger-than-life character. A hard worker with a strong set of principles, she would sooner leave a job than have her morals or her ethics compromised, telling an employer where they could 'shove it' and going and starting a new job. I think she did that quite a few times.

Life must have been so hard for Mum, as it is for any single mother. She worked so hard at a number of different jobs while battling illness, loneliness and despair. When I was three, she was unable to afford a baby-sitter, so she would take me to her night job, doing up the printing labels at the cold storage company where my grandfather was a computer programmer, and she would snuggle me up in a sleeping bag with a pillow under her desk. The drone of the old, heavy-duty printing machines would send me off to the Land of Nod like an industrial lullaby. There I'd be in my cocoon beneath the clattering machines, dozing and grizzling as she toiled on her labels until the early hours of the morning. When her shift was over, she would gently pick me up, trying not to wake me, and she would carry me home; and after tucking me into my bed, she would finally collapse into bed herself. Still today when I stick my earplugs in to go to sleep at night, I can hear cicadas and the low hum of printers.

Before he was a computer programmer, my grandfather was a high school maths and science teacher. My grandmother was a primary school teacher. When I was 5, Grandad gave me my own computer, a second-hand one. He created a DOS program of different computer games and taught me how to execute all the necessary DOS commands, which, considering the computer on which I wrote this book, now seems to have come from the stone age. My favourite game was *One Must Fall*, in which scary robots battled each other to the death. It had the cheesy graphics of the era, with pixelated explosions, positively 8-bit by today's standards, but I was obsessed. I was so entrenched in the fantasy that I was afraid of everyone I didn't know, suspecting that they might be an evil spy from Jupiter's moon Ganymede, where the game was set.

Money was a perennial problem for my mother. There never seemed to be enough to make ends meet. The following year, when Mum and I were living at our simply furnished but comfy Camp Hill flat, she received a nasty letter from the electricity company threatening that they were going to disconnect our power because she hadn't paid the bill. Mum simply didn't have the money at that time, and she went into the electricity company's office and told them that. She promised that she would lay her hands on the funds, somehow, and asked them if it would be all right if she paid the outstanding bill in a couple of days. The company said that they supposed that would be all right, but that the unpaid bill was not all that she was up for. In addition to the electricity bill, she would have to pay a disconnection fee, a bond and a reconnection fee. 'But the electricity hasn't been disconnected,' Mum quite reasonably protested. No matter, they came back, it was company policy when a bill hadn't been paid to charge penalty fees to compensate the company for the inconvenience. Unless they were paid, the power would be shut off. Mum hit the roof at this injustice. 'I'll pay the bill but there is no way I'm paying disconnection and reconnection fees when nothing has been disconnected,' she said. 'I'm daring you. I'm a single mother of a small boy. Why don't you go right ahead and turn off the power.' Later, pounding away on *One Must Fall*, I was alarmed when I learned about her angry conversation with the electricity company. My fears were justified. Next day, a man in a grey jacket came and cut off our electricity. My computer faded to black. The robots, at least, must have heaved a sigh of relief.

Of course, all Mum had to do was pay those unfair penalty fees and everything would have gone on as before, but – and I say good on her – she refused on principle. As far as this proud woman was concerned, being plunged into darkness and not being able to use any of our appliances was a small price to pay when she had a point to prove and she believed that right was on her side. That's so Vivienne. She's a real Taurus: stubborn and quite happy to go to extreme measures for the sake of a principle. Or upon reflection, perhaps it had a lot to do with the Asperger's she was diagnosed with only a few years ago, a condition that we've discovered runs through our genealogy.

Mum and I lived for six months without electricity. We had no electric lights, no electric hot water in the kitchen or bathroom, no TV or radio, no CD player, no electric jug, no toaster … no computer. It felt kind of medieval. Thank goodness our stove was powered by gas. Mum illuminated the house with candles. From a vintage store in New Farm she got her hands on a big candelabra that cast what can only be described as a romantic glow on the walls and ceiling of our little dining room and on our faces as we ate our regular evening fare of takeaway vegetarian pizza (she has been vegetarian since she was 14 … very strong principles!).

Mum reminded me recently that during this dark period of our lives I came home from school and told her that one of the kids had told her parents that she wished she could eat dinner like the Mitchams.

Mum said, 'What? Pizza every night?'

'No,' I replied, 'by candlelight, silly.'

Mum boiled water on the gas stove, one saucepan at a time, and filled our big bronze claw-footed bath tub just deep enough to accommodate me. Mum became a specialist in quick baths. Because we had no refrigerator, Grandad gave us ice bricks for the non-functioning freezer, and we were able to keep our milk and butter from going rancid that way. Our electricity-less half year took in autumn and winter. On the dwindling hot days we played with the garden hose in the back yard; these were the days before water restrictions. When it got chilly at night we went to bed early and buried down deep under the blankets. For entertainment we made do with an ancient wind-up gramophone complete with an outsized horn. I don't know how Mum came by that – she probably got it from the same place where she acquired the claw-footed bath, because they were both about the same ancient vintage. Mum put on a 78 record, wound up the gramophone with its crank handle, the record would spin, and from out of the horn would crackle:

Five foot two, eyes of blue,
But oh! what those five feet could do,
Has anybody seen my gal?

There were other records, but that's the song I remember. Mum adored it, and she encouraged me to sing along. Even today, 'Five Foot Two' can whisk me back to that little flat with purple and green stained-glass windows and no electricity. When I picked up the ukulele sixteen years later, I found the chords to that song so I could surprise Mum and indulge in a little bit of nostalgia.

The guy who disconnected our power was sent out to our house three more times by his boss to make sure that Mum hadn't illegally reconnected the electricity herself. And when she returned to the office half a year later to have the power put back on, she didn't end up having to pay the disconnection and reconnection fees, and the bond got reduced – so, you know, her stubbornness ended up sort of working in the end.

It was no fun at the time, and I especially hated not having my computer, but today surviving those six powerless months and being able to make the best of it together is among Mum's and my loveliest memories. I think she got a kick out of being a rebel and sticking it to the powers that be. It wouldn't be the last time she stood up to authority, on her own and my behalf.

Usually my mum was resilient and just got on with things, accepting struggling on a shoestring as her lot in life, but there were times when her sadness and frustration, the physical and emotional illnesses that dogged her, and sheer bone-tiredness got the better of her and she lashed out. Because many of the sources of her persecution were nameless voices at the end of a telephone line from the overdue payment division of whatever organisation, and I was always handy, usually she lashed out at me.

Mum screamed at me and smacked me, and while I never, ever for a moment stopped loving her, I was terrified of her. I always felt like I was going to get in trouble, no matter what I did. When I was in the car, I used to sit on the very edge of my seat, as far away as possible from Mum – or anybody, really – because I was afraid of doing something wrong and getting smacked. It was a nauseating feeling to be so jumpy.

She accepts now that I was never an especially naughty or unpleasant child. In fact, I was mostly a sweet and gentle little boy, as my doting grandma will happily attest to anyone who asks. But my mother had never developed coping mechanisms to deal with the stress and anger she felt. At times, facing difficult circumstances, everything bubbled up inside Mum. Whether I'd done something mischievous or nothing at all, I was her most accessible target, and she took it out on me. She was also being a stern mum for my own good, she says. She believed that she needed to control me and teach me right from wrong so I wouldn't run off the rails when I grew up; instilling fear in me would keep me from being bad. Maybe so. I am pretty sure that at the core of her behaviour was her brave battle to provide for us. At around age 5, to deprive her of reasons to chastise me, I adopted my lifelong self-preservation mechanism of lying to avoid getting into trouble. Sometimes with Mum it worked; usually she saw right through me.

Mum spent a lot of days sleeping. She often worked late and was exhausted, and she suffered from chronic fatigue syndrome. Perhaps, too, for her sometimes, unconsciousness was preferable to being awake. She also suffered severely when 'Aunty Flo' came to visit each month. If I made noise and woke her, she would go off her brain. I read a lot when I was little, because reading is a silent pastime. I would be severely and painfully roused on if I played the piano or watched TV with the sound up, and heaven help me if I threw or bounced balls.

I was alone a lot. Our neighbourhood in Camp Hill seemed to me to be a place where lots of old people lived, but few kids. Although a handful of playmates visited me occasionally, mostly the children there were macho and rough and not ones I wanted to play with. One day when I was 6, the 12-year-old neighbour of my aunt asked me to come to his shed. I went there with him and he did sexual things to me. Although I had little understanding of what had happened, I remember being jealous when not long afterwards I saw this same boy in his shed with another, older kid. When I went in to see what was going on he told me to go away, and I felt abandoned and bereft.

With few playmates, I lived inside my own head. I was my own best friend. Animals replaced human friends in my childhood. When I was 6, I had a mouse in a cage. Unless she was around to keep watch, Mum wouldn't let me touch the mouse, let alone play with it or pick it up, fearing I'd be too heavy-handed and kill it. She knew me well. Early one morning, I peeked into Mum's room and she was asleep. I couldn't resist. I crept to the mouse's cage and picked it up, and the little grey critter bit me on the finger. Its tiny razor-sharp teeth broke the skin. I yelped and dropped the mouse, which escaped. Blood from the bite was trickling down my hand and arm. I ran to the loo to wrap my lacerated finger in toilet paper so Mum couldn't see the wound. I thought if kept my hand in my pocket I just might be able to get away with it. But no. When Mum woke, one of the first things she saw was a trail of blood droplets from the mouse's cage to the toilet. She saw my guilty expression and tissue-wrapped finger. And she saw the empty mouse cage. Then she smacked me hard.

I didn't have a lot of luck with my pets. Nor, it must be said, did they have much luck with me. It was illegal to keep rabbits as pets in Queensland in the '90s because the authorities were concerned that they would escape from their pens and breed, and the state would be overrun by bunnies as well as cane toads. Grandma, however, knew her beloved grandson adored rabbits and brought two back for me from a trip. I named the grey one Sniffy and the black one Snuffy. I loved those rabbits to death. Literally. I just didn't know how to treat them and thought they were more durable than they were. One day I was playing with Sniffy on the couch, just chucking him gently onto a cushion, pretending that he was Superman. He would bounce on the cushion and his legs would fling out and I thought that was so cute. I had no idea that throwing Sniffy like this was not good for him. I picked him up in my hands for one more Superman flight and he did a wee on my hand and went limp and lay still. I had broken Sniffy's neck. I was horrified and distraught. So was Snuffy, who skittered up and sadly rubbed his nose in Sniffy's tiny pool of wee. I gave

Sniffy a solemn burial ceremony, with Snuffy and me the principal, and only, mourners. I put the dear departed rabbit in a shoebox and buried him under the mulberry tree in the back yard. I cried my heart out. Today Mum and I can see the funny side of Sniffy's tragic demise. We say that Sniffy snuffed it and Snuffy sniffed it. Black humour, I suppose.

Of course, when Mum demanded to know what had happened to Sniffy, I told her I had no idea, because I didn't want to be punished. 'He just died, Mum,' I said. 'Honest.' In my childhood, and my teenage years, when I was regularly landing in strife for doing things that were much worse than picking up a rodent or even murdering Sniffy, I lied a lot. Sometimes I told falsehoods not even to save my skin, just for the sake of lying. It was my first instinct. A few years ago, after some traumatic events brought me undone, I concluded that honesty in every aspect of my life is the only policy, so I don't lie any more. Writing this book would have been much easier had I never made such a decision.

My mum has since apologised for terrifying me. Though she beats herself up about her parenting methods, I know that she was doing her best, doing the only thing she knew how to do. The best, and only, light I can put on our relationship is that, in the end, I turned out all right, and so has she. Today Mum and I are more best friends than mother and son. Some of my friends think that's weird. It works for us.

My grandma taught me to read and write when I was 4. 'Pat and Sam ... see Pat run ... watch Pat jump.' She would make little word cards – cat, tree, ball – and pin them to the curtain and I'd connect the picture with the word. She would put the cards on a table in a certain order and I would look at them and write a sentence: the boy with the ball is with a cat in the tree, that kind of thing. She was a wonderful teacher. When I started kindergarten I was the only child already able to read. My first school was Belmont Kindergarten, and then from the age of 5, for Years 1 to 6, I attended Our Lady of Mount Carmel Catholic Primary School in Coorparoo. There was a church and a nuns' convent on the large grounds. The nuns would tie a ribbon on the handrail of the main staircase in the school to indicate that the church was open at lunchtime for kids to pray. There was much Bible reading throughout the week. Each classroom had a little altar, and every week a student was rostered to decorate it with religious figures and flowers, whatever came to hand that seemed appropriate. When we pupils saw a teacher for the first time every day or if a new teacher appeared in our classroom, we had been instructed to address them with, 'Good morning, Miss Apostolos' – or whatever the teacher's name happened to be – 'and peace be with you.' The teachers were strict – though never as strict as Mum! – and the children were consequently well-behaved. I never really enjoyed the religious instruction at Mount Carmel, but the stories from the Bible took me to bygone days and far-off lands.

Mum had a close friend, Pauline, who married a deaf man, and through Pauline and her husband she met a number of people who had impaired hearing or no hearing. So she could have conversations with her friends, Mum learned sign language, and for a bit she even worked as a volunteer interpreter in the deaf community. Because she couldn't afford a babysitter when she went to sign language classes at night, she took me along with her. I was about 7. If I wasn't colouring in the Bs and Ds in my homework book, I would be watching and learning as the instructor taught the class to use sign language. Before long I knew the signs. One evening the instructor took me by the hand and led me to the front of the community centre hall and stood me on a table in front of everyone. I signed, 'My name is Matthew,' and then finger spelled M-A-T-T-H-E-W. Everyone – including Mum, who had no idea I was paying attention to the lessons – was suitably impressed.

Back at home, my mum and I often communicated with each other in sign language. I had always got into trouble from her if I interrupted her while she was on the phone to ask her if I could have this or that or go to one place or another, so signing allowed me to ask her things without breaking in. She would cradle the phone between her shoulder and cheek to free her hands, and give me a sign language yes or a no while continuing to chat away. Later, when I was diving, our sign language allowed us to speak to each other from afar, Mum in the grandstand and me high up on the diving platform.

Mum made sure that I held no grudge against my father for leaving us behind by never once saying anything negative about him. Knowing that my father and I would surely meet one day, she didn't want to taint my opinion of him. She wanted me to form my own opinion. In fact, she told me often, 'Your sporting prowess is thanks to your father's genes, not mine, and we should thank him for that, and that surely wherever he is he is proud of what you have achieved'.

I think, too, that she refused to be critical of my father because she feared I might transfer bad feelings about him to myself or convince myself that by being born I was responsible for their break-up.

Mum kept a photograph of my father that was taken during their brief relationship (and which she later told me she nicked from him!). He is lying on the sand at the beach and grinning cheekily at the camera. He looks very fit and bursting with good health, and has a pleasant, open face and mousy brown hair, like mine, and it is about the same length that mine is now, and bleached at the tips by the Queensland sun. One day when I was 12, I jumped out of the water at the pool at Belmont. My mum and grandma were there at poolside watching me, and as I launched myself like a seal out of the water, drenching everyone, I was smiling broadly, and they both gave a double-take and remarked that I had my father's grin. There are pictures in Grandma's and Mum's photo albums of me when I was a boy. I was small and slight of frame, sandy-haired, and wore the usual Queensland kids' outfit of shorts, singlet and thongs. In most of these childhood photographs I'm pulling a funny face, sticking my tongue out, popping my eyes. It was a habit I had whenever anyone produced a camera. It's a habit that I've never outgrown.

Never having had a dad, I didn't miss him. I felt no sense of loss or abandonment. Mum and her mother and father were enough. But from time to time when I was growing up, I would find myself wondering what kind of man Greg was. Although Mum was always open about him, I guess I didn't feel comfortable asking her too much. She was a sensitive soul, and I was always afraid of what kind of response I would receive.

Once when I was 7, I found a letter documenting a child support payment from my father to my mother, and it contained his full name and phone number, so I got out the White Pages and I traced him to an address in Brisbane. I found two sets of initials, so deduced that he was now married, and I made up that he had a number of children, my step-siblings. I didn't call his phone number, or go to see where he lived. I didn't dare. I didn't want to disrupt his life or open old wounds. And I didn't want Mum to find out I'd been playing amateur detective and sneaking around behind her back. Deep down, I knew that my father and I would meet one day, but I didn't want that day to come until I was much older. Even as a little boy, I knew that I would not be wise or emotionally mature enough to cope with the situation. I put my father on the backburner ...

Because my grandparents were former teachers, there were always books in their homes, and it was natural that a lonely and easily bored 7-year-old like me would pick them up and let them whisk him away to new worlds. Best of all those volumes were the *World Book Encyclopedias*. I devoured the facts and figures that their musty pages contained. Reading them cover to cover was my favourite thing to do. I was never more blissfully happy than when sitting on the toilet with an open encyclopedia perched on my bare and bony knees. I spent hours on the loo, because I was alone and felt safe there. No subject in the encyclopedia was too arcane, obscure or difficult – they all fascinated me. I was especially entranced by spiders and snakes, maybe because they creeped me out. (They still do.) I also learned the capital city of every state in America, along with each state's bird, land mass and population. I tried to do the same thing for all the countries in the world. Another obsession of mine was vexillology: I knew every country's flag. My favourite was the Nepalese flag because it was the only one that wasn't rectangular. It has two red triangles, one on top of the other, with a white symbol in each.

On my way to the toilet I'd ask Mum to give me a subject, any subject, to read up on, and by the time that I emerged I'd practically be an expert on the matter. I know it's odd, not to say unhygienic, that I spent so much time on the loo, but Mum and Grandma were cool with it because they knew what I was doing there.

One time Mum had a friend over to our place and we were all watching TV's *Sale of the Century*, having fun trying to answer quiz master Tony Barber's questions before the contestants could press their buttons. This particular evening, Tony asked, 'Where would you find the Jacobson organ?' The poor contestants didn't have a clue. Nor did Mum and her pal. But I did, and piped up, 'It's on the roof of a snake's mouth. It helps the snake smell'.

Mum said, 'Yes, sure, sweetheart'. She turned to her friend and they had a quiet chuckle.

Mum stopped laughing – in fact, her jaw just about hit the floor – when Tony Barber gave the answer, 'The Jacobson organ is in a snake's head'.

And furthermore, I proceeded to point out, my answer was more specific than Tony's.

Every now and then, I recall obscure facts, and it's due to reading those *World Book Encyclopedias* when I was a kid. There's no doubt in my mind that part of the romance of those heavy and awkward books was that they gave me knowledge to escape from the world I lived in.

I was a sponge, absorbing and retaining everything I read. My grandma tells me I knew the names of every child in my kindergarten when I was 4, and I loved learning to read and speak French and Italian at school. My grandma still marvels at my ability at age 5 to be playing a board game and throw the dice and move my piece straight to the correct square on the board in a flash and without counting out loud. I just knew immediately where it had to go. It was an innate ability I seemed to have to take in information and then have my body react instantly and without me thinking about it. My mind ran at a million miles an hour when I was a kid. I thought about things deeply, critically and analytically, and was as philosophical as a kid can be about what was happening in my life. I stressed over why things were the way they were and how I wanted them to be. I couldn't turn this overdrive thinking off.

There had never been any acrimony between my grandmother and grandfather after they separated, and both of them were always in my life. Grandad would still come over to mow Grandma's lawn or fix her computer and things like that. Sometimes I would play gin rummy and zilch and other board games and card games with Grandad and his partner – but as I got older, work took up more of his time, and for a while he lived in Boston setting up computer systems for the company he worked for.

With Mum often at work, asleep or unwell, Grandma would look after me. I liked to tie one end of a skipping rope to a handrail and persuade her to take the other end and turn the rope for me while I jumped over it for hours on end. An indication that I was a bit different, perhaps? The poor woman had to keep changing arms because her shoulders got so sore. Bless her.

At school I had a few friends, but formed no deep bonds. There was one kid I considered to be my best friend. We hung out together more than we did with other kids, but now all I can remember about him is that he loved Green Day. I really didn't get along with a few of the boys, which might have had something to do with my preference for singing in the choir at lunchtime and skipping with the girls rather than playing rugby, soccer or cricket. I was considered a little odd, eccentric and girly. When I decided to give footy a go, I did my best to run and tackle, yet was invariably the last kid picked. And fair enough, because I was rubbish at footy, and in fact at all team sports. What I was good at was the post-goal celebrations, doing rows of flips from one end of the oval to the other. (I didn't really make it hard for anyone to guess, did I?) Swimming, ironically, when you think of all the time I would spend in pools in the years to come, was another sport I sucked at. All I was good at was jumping, skipping and flipping.

So, I was a solitary little boy, afraid of his mum's temper, picked on at school because I was different, always reading voraciously in the loo, on my bed or lying prone in the backyard, dreaming and scheming in my own world. I was desperate to prove that everyone who was mean and laughed at me was wrong about me and that I was the best in the world at something. Then, I was sure, people would like me.

The only problem was that I had no idea what my field of excellence would be. I would find something ...

2

my first true love

It was a great day when I got my own trampoline. Grandad's girlfriend had an old rusty-framed Olympic-sized tramp with jagged holes in it and no safety pads – a far cry from those springless, netted trampolines kids get these days. The trampoline was the girlfriend's son's, but he had grown up and didn't use it any more. She thought I might like it. I instantly approved of her from that point forwards (a testament to how fickle children can be). Somehow, that trampoline was manhandled into our backyard in Camp Hill, and in no time it had become my favourite thing in the world. You couldn't get me off it. I was amazed when Mum taught me how to do seat drops, where you bounce on your bottom on the trampoline and spring back up onto your feet. Mum, I am still learning to this day, has many surprising attributes. Soon I was bouncing high into the sky and doing seat drops and back flips. One day, after I'd said, 'Mum, look at me,' five dozen times and she'd finally relented, she was actually amazed when I performed 13 back flips in a row. I didn't stop at 13. It became a challenge every day to see how many consecutive back flips I could do before I fell off the trampoline or got so dizzy that I vomited.

When the next-door neighbours' kids occasionally did come to my place for a bounce on my trampoline, we played a game called Egg. We all got up onto the trampoline and took turns curling ourselves into a ball, and then the others would bounce the 'egg' higher and higher while the target of their attention would see how long he or she could retain the egg shape. It was a dangerous game because the egg often bounced right off the tramp onto the ground and 'broke'.

The trampoline, like my pets – at least those that survived – accompanied me to all the places I lived. One time when Mum was having a down period and thought it best if I went to stay with my grandma for a bit, I jumped so high and so hard that I shot off the trampoline backwards and smashed into a tree and, damned near unconscious, slid like a character in a cartoon down its trunk and lay in a heap on the ground, gasping and groaning. I had bark cuts and scratches all over my back and I had winded myself. When I tried to scream for Grandma to come and help me, no sound came out except a wheeze. Luckily a neighbour had heard the thwack when I collided with the tree, and she ran to alert my grandmother, who, as she always did when I came to grief of one kind or another, came running. She cleaned me up, and eventually the air returned to my lungs. Of course, the moment it did, I jumped right back onto the trampoline. I tumbled off that rusty old contraption more times than I can remember. I was fearless.

Mum and Grandma thought it was a good idea for me to take trampoline lessons before I broke my neck. It was February 1997 and I was 8 when I started going to classes at Robertson Gymnastics Club. My first trampoline instructor was a friend of Mum's named Steve Bland, who was the head coach then and went on to perform with the Cirque du Soleil acrobatic show in Las Vegas. Later my coach was Natalie Abreu (now Gillis), who had won gold, silver and bronze medals in the World Trampoline Championships.

For all its funding and infrastructure challenges, trampolining is a surprisingly big sport. In terms of the number of participants at elite levels, it is much bigger than diving. Each year at the Australian Trampoline Championships, the Queensland team alone would always consist of more than a hundred athletes. There are four disciplines: individual trampoline, where the gymnast does two routines of ten consecutive skills; synchronised trampoline, where two gymnasts perform the same routine at the same time on adjacent tramps; double-mini trampoline, in which you take a run-up and do tricks first off a small sloping tramp and then off an adjoining horizontal tramp; and tumbling, which is like the floor in gymnastics, but is performed on a runway 25 metres long and two metres wide.

Many people refuse to take trampolining seriously because they equate it with a bunch of kids bouncing up and down on a battered tramp, like the one I used to have, in the backyard. In truth, it is incredibly technically demanding at the top level. (I watched the finals of the trampoline events at the Beijing Olympics. I had always believed that when my diving career was over I would return to the trampoline, but after seeing how the sport has progressed I realised I would never return. At my age I could never attain the required level of excellence.)

In my early days at Robertson Gymnastics, there were times when I wondered if the trampoline was really for me. What I was being taught was vastly more difficult and complex than the simple stuff I loved to do on my backyard trampoline. There were not too many games of Egg at Robertson. I had a lot of trouble with my form, which, as I was just a novice, was sloppy. To begin with, I was a really ugly trampolinist, but I trained hard and got better.

In 1998, I began competing regularly in interclub and state and national competitions. I won gold medals at state meets; and at my first National Championships, in Melbourne in 1998, I won three silver medals, finishing second in the double-mini trampoline, synchronised trampoline and tumbling, and placing sixth in the trampoline.

I was at home on the trampoline. Unlike with any other sport I'd tried, here I was naturally athletic. I had innate balance and aerial awareness. I was good at the flipping and airborne acrobatics. Having no fear was another benefit; if I bounced right off the trampoline and crashed into a tree or to the ground I didn't care, as soon as I recovered I was back on the trampoline and jumping higher than ever and pushing myself to perfect another manoeuvre.

I was able to think about and memorise the routines and movements in a methodical, mathematical way. Just as I could bring to mind whole pages from the encyclopedia and hit the keys on my computer in certain DOS combinations when playing *One Must Fall*, I devised a systematic way of remembering my trampoline moves, sequentially and mathematically interlacing the complex components of a routine. (Later, I memorised the twists, turns and contortions of the complicated, high-scoring dives on my dive list the same way.) I had found my first sporting niche.

Today when I do my speaking engagements, I start off by telling the story of the ugly duckling: me. 'Little Matty wasn't good at sports, he never fit in. He tried soccer, rugby, cricket, swimming and running and was always picked last for team sports. He never won a blue ribbon at the swimming or athletics carnivals. He was just a skinny kid with knobbly knees, too clumsy to fit in. He always felt rejected and dejected. He had just about decided that if he was ever going to realise his dream to be the best in the world at something, that something was not going to be a sport. Then, one day, he was given a trampoline. Turns out he was actually good at trampolining. One thing led to another and, to his surprise, in 2008 he ended up being the Olympic champion in diving. The moral of Little Matty's story is: If at first you don't succeed, try, try, try and try again! You don't have to be the fittest, smartest or strongest to be the best or even successful. The key is to find a niche, an activity, a community where you fit in. Trampolining and then diving happened to be my niche.'

My trampoline more than compensated for my isolated existence, for having no close friends and for Mum always being at work. I could spend hours on the tramp even if I was all by myself. Who needed mates? Suddenly, being alone was not so bad. I could express and challenge myself on my trampoline, and bouncing high and doing my moves I felt free and exhilarated. Jumping and tumbling also was an antidote to the moods that were increasingly creeping up on me and dragging me down.

I liked to loosely tie a bed sheet to the trampoline's springs, then jump and see the sheet fluff up like a big white marshmallow parachute. I would land on my back on the billowing sheet and let it envelop me. It was magical. When in the mood, I would lie on the mat, feeling it gently pulsate under my weight, and gaze at the sky searching for shapes in the clouds scurrying overhead.

Later, in 1997, when I was 9 and Mum gave birth to my brother, Marcus, we moved to the Brisbane suburb of Wakerley to live with Marcus's father, who was a boyfriend of my mum. I joined the nearby Wynnum PCYC at Lota, where my trampoline coach was Melanie Tonks, who coached Ji Wallace, the silver medallist at the Olympic Games in Sydney in 2000.

Melanie could not have been more different in her manner than the quiet, friendly and mild-mannered Natalie Abreu. They were both fine instructors, but Melanie, who had frizzy purple hair, was bossy and, a bit like Mum, controlled kids by instilling fear. She could really shout loudly for one so tiny. It's not that she was a nasty person — in fact, she could be really funny, and her bark was much worse than her bite. She just knew that she got results by being cranky and autocratic with her pupils. As soon as she pointed her finger and opened her mouth it was business. In spite of her prickly manner, she was, and is, well respected and her athletes love her. Whenever she wanted to introduce us to a new, complex sequence of moves, she used to like to trick us into doing it. If she wanted us to start performing some quite scary new skill, like multiple twisting double somersaults, she would break down the sequence into individual parts that were easier and much less intimidating. She would make us do those parts over and over again, and once we had been lulled into thinking it wasn't hard, she would tell us to just put all the individual parts together, so suddenly we were doing this complicated sequence of moves. Or she would get us doing a sequence over and over and then suddenly spring on us that we had to add a somersault at the end. It was her way of getting around our mental blocks and resistance. But early on I always knew what was coming, and she would grumble, 'Why can't you just be stupid like the other kids?' It was when I trained with Melanie that I really blossomed as a trampolinist.

My grandma and grandad were not flush with funds yet selflessly paid for my trampoline coaching and funded my trips to compete in championships. Mum took out loans as well. I owe them all a huge debt.

In 1999, I had my first overseas trip – to the Trampoline World Age Games, held at the holiday resort of Sun City, just outside of Johannesburg, South Africa. I placed 20-something on the individual trampoline, 13th on the double-mini and 9th in tumbling. Travelling overseas was a revelation. All my experience of other people and other lands was vicarious, gained through encyclopedias or TV. Now I was seeing the big wide world for myself, and it was fabulous and, I now realised, a lot bigger than Brisbane. My grandad paid for my trip, and my grandma paid to come along as my chaperone. To this 11-year-old, Sun City was the most exotic place on earth. Our hotel had its own animal park and backed onto a massive lake where guests para-sailed. There was an enormous wave pool where the water built up behind a wall and rushed down into the pool in a massive wave when the floodgate was opened every 20 minutes or so. The pool's 90-foot drop water slides were claimed to be the fastest and hairiest in the world, and I had ride after ride. When you hit the bottom, your arms and legs go flying. No matter how tight you try to keep your body, you end up a hurtling tangle of spaghetti. You get the ultimate mega wedgie as well! They even had in-ground trampolines and giant chessboards with chess pieces the size of adults. It was surreal.

The trampolining competition was held in a Super Bowl surrounded by a vast shopping centre. Afterwards we went to Kruger National Park to see the lions, elephants, baboons with the big red bums and other wildlife. The eating areas were outdoors and monkeys jumped up on the tables and grabbed packets of sugar and ran back up to the trees, easily evading the waiters who frantically tried to chase them away with brooms. It was hilarious. Seeing animals up close was so much better than in pictures in books or on television. Unlike my computer games, travelling was a real, not a virtual, experience. I didn't need exploding robots to have an unforgettable time.

There were no monkeys or water slides, but the Australian state and national junior trampoline championships where I competed were a lot of fun, too. There were around 100 athletes in the Queensland team, and competitions were usually staged in Rockhampton, Gosford or Melbourne. I was one of the top junior trampolinists in Australia, but there was little chance of me getting carried away with myself. Because there was no official funding, trampolining scraped by on the goodwill of the administrators, the participants and their families and friends who were always reaching into their own pockets. There were some novel ways of raising funds, and my grandma was always involved. A group of parents made bags to sell, plain canvas bags with the logo of the competition on the front. Hard to imagine, but nobody bought them. So one of the mums went to the nearest Spotlight store and bought dozens of cushion inserts, and the other mums turned the unpopular canvas satchels into super-cool signature cushions that sold like hotcakes.

When I was at Wynnum PCYC everyone would pitch in to hire a bus or, more likely, a van to take us to events in Queensland and interstate, and the driver would be one of the dads. It was anything but luxurious. We were all crammed in together. There was never a toilet on the bus. It was a race to board first so we could put our mat in the aisle or between the seats so we could stretch out and sleep. Those were long drives and the bus was really uncomfortable. We brought kilos of lollies and stuffed our faces. That was a form of team bonding, I suppose. When we arrived we would take over the cheap motel we'd have been booked into. There was lots of noisy running in the motel corridors and hanging out in each other's rooms. It was so much fun, and that's why my heart was in it. I was doing the sport because I loved it.

Trampolining made me feel part of a strong and supportive community. For the first time in my life I felt like I *belonged*. I enjoyed and was challenged by the sport. I liked the people who were involved. In the trampolining community I felt popular. I even had girlfriends. Mum recently found a stash of letters from trampoline girls written on coloured paper with puppy dogs all over them. The girls were either upset that I had broken up with them, or telling me that they were breaking up with me because we lived thousands of kilometres apart and they just couldn't do the long-distance thing any more.

When I was 15, I summoned up the courage to confess to Mum that I was gay. She had seen some gay porn on my computer. At first I told her I was bi, then I conceded that

I was gay. Her response? '*Derrr*! I've known that for years.' Looking back, it would have been unusual if she had not seen the signs. There was the skipping with girls and the parading around in Grandma's clothes and makeup. When I was 7 or 8 and I was at Grandma's being looked after for the day, I went into her sewing room, where she kept all of the clothes she hadn't worn for years. I dressed up, put on one of her old wigs and some high heels, then used her makeup so I could go out and surprise her and make her laugh. I did myself up like a Spice Girl, but in a real parody-like way, with garishly blue eye shadow and really bright red lipstick and heavy rouge circles on my cheeks. There was no coordination in the outfit whatsoever: a hideous floral print boob tube with a white micro mini and an ugly brown curly wig. That white micro mini I found in Grandma's sewing room just completely blew my mind. It totally contradicted the image I had of her. And I couldn't get my head around how it would have fit her, because when I put it on – even with my little hips – my junk was hanging out the bottom of it in my undies. When I came out of the sewing room, Grandma thought it was absolutely hilarious – which is why she kept letting me do it whenever I went over there for the day.

But there was probably no bigger giveaway than my lurid trampolining leotards. Grandma made them to my strict specifications after we went together to Spotlight to buy

Apparently I've always been quite comfortable being wet and (relatively) nude.

Mum and grandma look really tired.
Maybe because it took them 26 hours to get me out?

Once a waterbaby,
always a waterbaby.
Learning to swim
with mum at
Hollins Swim
School in Brisbane

The only photo I have of my dad growing up, which mum recently revealed she actually pinched from him! How great is his hair?!

Same outfit, 30 years later. My uncle Lenny and I, both aged 3.

Pretty good technique for a three-year-old. My head just needs to be a little smaller.

I had Justin Bieber hair before it was cool. (With my puppy Annabella.)

My first day of school.
Everyone called me
Harry for some reason …

The rickety old rust bucket given to me by granddad's girlfriend. I approved of
her from that point onwards. And this is how my trampolining career started.

On trampoline 2.0 with my little brother, Marcus. Carina, 1999.

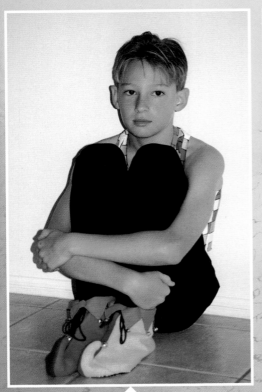

Grandma also made most of my leotards for trampolining. The purple velvet beauty in the middle is what I won my World Age title in.

A shy jester, how ironic. Grandma made my outfit for Medieval Week at school, complete with jingling jester hat.

Quite the ladies' man at the Trampoline World Age Games, South Africa 1999 …

… oh, who am I kidding? I was as camp as a row of tents!

Marvellous Matthew

TRAMPOLINING

MOVE over Ji Wallace and Robyn Forbes — Wynnum PCYC has another world-class trampoline champion. Gumdale's Matthew Mitcham followed in the footsteps of his PCYC predecessors by winning gold at the World Age Championships in Denmark.

Mitcham, 13, won the world title in the 13-14 years double mini trampoline event, beating 55 other competitors. Mitcham has represented Queensland three times at nationals, winning three silver medals in 1998, two silvers and a bronze in 1999 and two gold and two silver in 2000.

"I expected him to make the top 20 and would've been happy with that," coach Melanie Tonks said. "He's doing more now than Ji (Wallace) at this age."

● Matthew Mitcham — world champion at the age of 13.

BM2407

In the local paper, the *Wynnum Herald,* after winning World Age Games in 2001. The photo does not do justice to the sparkly purple velvet leotard. Little did I know that grandma had been collating a scrapbook of every little article I was ever in over the years. Scrapbooking. It's a dying art.

'Bound for glory in Germany', the headline on an article that appeared with this photo in the *South-East Advertiser* after winning three golds at the 2002 National Diving Championships, and qualifying for my first Junior World Championships for diving, one year after winning gold at the Trampoline World Age Games.

This photo of me in action accompanied a *South-East Advertiser* cover article in 2005, reporting the three gold (and one silver) medals I won at the 2005 Youth Olympic Festival, making me the most successful athlete at that competition. However, the real reason I included this picture is because it is the only action shot of me in existence in which I don't look constipated, which is a good enough reason in itself.

I pierced my tongue at 14 – an act of teenage rebellion. This is my friend Nikky. She was the token lesbian at our school – out and proud from day dot, and universally liked and respected for it.

I dyed my hair black at 15 to reflect my teenage angst. Eventually I ditched the dye but kept the piercing.

Being a knob at a party organised by Open Doors, a youth service for LGBT (Lesbian, Gay, Bisexual, Transgender) teenagers. It's a wonderful organisation that offers a safe place for young people to be themselves and meet peers. It also provides counselling and other services for those in need. I spent a lot of time there throughout my high school years and am extremely grateful to have had this available to me.

Another one from grandma's scrapbook. This picture was taken on the oval at Mansfield State High School just before the Commonwealth Games in 2006. I had two people hold the flag taut in the background while I ran up and did a round-off into a backsault in front of it to achieve this picture. Who needs Photoshop?

My last real stab at having a girlfriend, mixtapes and all. Martina and I now joke that she turned me gay – a badge she wears with pride!

My French Immersion class performed a play at Southbank in Year 11 for Bastille Day. I, of course, volunteered to be the 'Fat Lady'.

Gay   Christian   D'uh   Straight

I had quite a colourful little clique at school. Most of my friends were musos. This is a few of my closest friends, Kirk, Dani and Jess, with whom I spent so much time throughout my teens that their families adopted me as their own.

© Photograph by Douglas Cairns

While I joke about how demoralising clown diving may seem, the money I got for diving into that tiny tank was a godsend. My employers, the Flying Lotahs Aquaworld, were even good enough to advance me half the money because I couldn't afford the train to and from Olympic Park each day.

For all you honeys out there, I'm your 'Super Bee'.

I met Lachlan and my two besties Shane and Lexi all around the same time in 2006. The timing coincides with coming out of the 'dark ages' of my teenage years. **So. Much. Love.**

Alex Croak and I having some pre-competition funsies, Beijing 2008.

Sexiest. Olympians

This fab four are toned, honed and among the best athletes in the world

Named as part of *WHO* mag's Sexiest of 2008. Being cynical, I asked if they were just being PC by including the 'gay Olympian' but they assured me they named me for my body. Which is fair enough.

the lycra ... I had a pair in blue snake-skin; another in pink snake-skin; a pair with random purple, red, orange and white checks. I was the most garishly dressed young trampolinist in Brisbane, and didn't I enjoy the attention! My leotards also came in handy at school when we had a semester dedicated to medieval times and I fronted as a court jester in my colourful trampoline leotards and a jester's cap with bells and curly-toed slippers, also made by my grandma. Other students dressed as kings and queens. It was typical of me to play the jester and be a show pony, doing my flips and handstands. I like an audience.

Mum, Marcus and I lived with Marcus's dad in Wakerley from the time I was 9 until I was 13, and I attended Gumdale State School. Things didn't work out, and we three went back to live in my grandfather's house in Carina. The trampoline, of course, came with us, and Mum gave away the 60 or more guinea pigs we had, which all had M names: Maisy, Mason, Mindy and Mandy (they were twins), Madison, Maya, Mariah, Maxine, Matilda, Milly, Molly, Myrtle, Mabel, Maggie, Melinda and so on and so forth.

I stumbled into diving by chance. It was the hot Brisbane summer of late 1999 and I was 11. I hung out a lot at the aquatic centre in the suburb of Chandler, which was built for the 1982 Commonwealth Games and was the headquarters of the Australian Institute of Sport Diving Program. The public was allowed to use the diving boards in the diving pool when the AIS squad was not training. This day I was showing off on the 1 metre board. While other kids were content to do massive bombs off it, I was doing double flips and then just as I was about to hit the water I tucked up my legs into the bomb position. *KER-SPLASH*! They were pretty spectacular bombs, I must say. Water went everywhere. A small crowd gathered to watch the show, and among them was the renowned AIS coach who was known as 'Mr Wong' (his real name is Wang Tong Xiang), who just happened to be walking along the pool deck. This elderly, distinctly menacing, Chinese man called out to me, 'Boy! Come over here!' I was terrified. I was expecting him to tell me off for being a dick and horsing around, but instead he said, 'How do you know how to do those dives?'

I replied, 'I'm a trampolinist'.

'Well,' said Mr Wong, 'Do you want to try diving?'

3

taking the plunge, and other diving puns

My diving career began the following week and I was soon made a member of the Australian Institute of Sport (AIS) Talent Identification Squad (or TID, because it seems you can never have too many acronyms in elite sport). The TID was a junior tier of the AIS diving program, for divers with the potential to be champions. The AIS diving program based itself at the pool at Chandler because it had the best diving facilities in Australia. Sharleen Stratton, who would win gold at the 2006 and 2010 Commonwealth Games and compete at the 2008 Beijing and 2012 London Olympics, was in the same group as me, and we've been friends to this day.

Diving was exciting and challenging and my prospects looked terrific, yet I had no intention when I took it up of quitting trampolining. I enjoyed trampolining too much. I saw no reason why I could not do both sports. I trained with the diving squad before and after school and then I trampolined at night.

My first diving coach was Li Kong Rong. 'K.R.', as he was known to us, had been one of China's best divers before coming to Australia to coach. China has long been the premier diving nation in the world, so the AIS hired China's coaches in a bid to bring Australian diving up to a similar standard, a strategy that's working. He was a smart and successful coach, and my confidence soared when he told me that my introduction to the sport was easier than most novices' because I came with in-built aerial awareness and I was fearless, both traits that cannot be coached. I guess aerial awareness was a product of trampolining. I never had qualms about launching myself off the 10 metre platform even before I knew how to enter the water correctly, and, believe me, you hit the water with considerable impact from that height. Today, more than a decade later, I'm a little more circumspect. Plunging from a great height is an occupational hazard of being a platform diver and occasionally I would think, just before I took off into space, 'What the flying nun am I doing?'

These days when I dive competitively, I go into the event with a set-in-stone list of dives that my coach and I have decided upon, based on my ability to perform them better than my rivals and their degree of difficulty (the more difficult the dive, the more points it is worth if you pull it off). But when I first started diving back in 1999 it was a case of mucking around on the boards, learning and experimenting, finding out what I was capable of.

I started out by doing what's called a peanut roll, a basic starter dive that all kids do when they begin training. I would sit on the edge of the springboard on my bottom and roll forward, entering the water hands first. I began on the 1 metre springboard and worked up to the 3 metre, 5 metre and 7½ metre. When we had five minutes of play time at the end of a training session, we'd all run to the 10 metre fixed platform – which has no spring, or 'give', in it – and take turns jumping off for fun, doing straight jumps like pin drops. Pretty soon I was ready to do peanut rolls off the 10 metre platform and was doing basic dives off the springboards.

I learned all the main types of dives: you could face the pool and after launching yourself into the air, somersault either forwards or backwards; you could take off from the board with your back to the water and, again, somersault either forwards or backwards; you could twist in mid-air; and from the 10 metre platform, you could even begin your dive from a handstand position on the edge, though it would be a while before I worked my way up to that. I also learned the basic body positions of competitive diving: the tuck, where you pull your thighs tightly to your chest and make sure your heels are close to your bum; the pike, where you keep your legs straight and bend only at the waist; and straight, in which you might slightly arch your back but otherwise don't bend your body.

The body positions are more or less the same in diving as in trampolining. The only thing I had to change was my pike position: I grabbed behind my knees rather than holding my ankles, making for a tighter pike.

Another similarity with trampolining is that diving also has a synchro event, in which two divers go through their dives simultaneously and are judged not only on how well each performs their dive but also how well they sync up.

When you jump forward off the board but somersault backwards, it's called a 'reverse' – and that is one of the scary dives, because you can't actually see where the board is when you're doing your rotation. Everyone who watched the Olympics in Seoul in 1988 knew the dangers of the reverse, as that was the dive in which Greg Louganis hit his head on the springboard and had to have stitches. But as an 11-year-old, I had an underdeveloped self-preservation mechanism, so the reverse didn't worry me. The dive that I did have some fear of was the 'inward', when you stand on the end of the board with your back to the water, launch yourself into the air backwards but somersault forwards, towards the board. The inward is quite hard to get right and requires a lot of accurate angles and really good timing; at first, I often went too close to the board, and I hit my feet a few times.

Out the back of the utilitarian concrete aquatic centre at Chandler was a big shed, which housed a dry-land diving training centre with in-ground trampolines, in-ground foam pits, dry boards and harnesses. I knew the Chandler dry-land centre well, because I had trained for trampoline there before I started diving, using the pit to learn new skills such as my multiple twisting double somersault. Around the pool, the grounds were thick bush and jungle where ducks, water hens and bush turkeys roamed about. I have a soft spot for ducks. As a warm-up, before endlessly performing our dives for our coaches, we had to complete a 2 kilometre run around the ring-road. We headed for the ponds, because there was a duck there we called Da. Da was fearless and came right up to us, unlike the other ducks, which scuttled away. Da talked to us. We'd say, 'Morning, Da,' and Da would come right back at us, 'Da, da!'

I hated running; it gave me shin splints. I was known to cut through a parking lot to knock a kilometre or so off the distance, and I wasn't alone. Then we'd partner stretch for 20 minutes, stretching the hamstrings, the adductors, the glutes, shoulders – all the main muscle groups. After that, in the dry land area we did dozens of somersaults onto mats, on trampolines, into foam pits, and more core-muscle exercises than you could poke a stick at. That was every day from 6am to 8am, Monday to Friday. Then Sharleen Stratton and I would shower and Grandma would take us to school. Every single morning she cooked us a hot breakfast, which we'd eat in the car on the way. Sharleen's mother would bring us back to the pool in the afternoon, and we'd train from about quarter past 3 until 6, then Grandma would pick me up and drive me to trampoline training. I never did a shred of homework.

I had a head start in my diving career because of my trampolining. I didn't have to learn how to do twists and turns in the air, because I could already do them. I just had to adapt them to diving into water rather than landing on the trampoline. Sure, I had to develop my flexibility, strength, form and discipline, but so did everybody else. In my armoury already was aerial awareness, and I could lock the sequence of movements of a dive into my brain and when it came time to perform it, let muscle memory take over. Mastering the skills you need for diving takes years, but I took to it as quickly as I did to trampolining and went full-on at both.

All the other kids in the Talent Identification Squad had been gymnasts or trampolinists too. Many kids are handpicked from those disciplines to become divers, because they tend to progress much faster through the sport than kids who come into diving cold. That's because kids tend to develop aerial awareness and learn somersaults much more quickly in gymnastics, because they train about five times a week even at the very start, while beginner divers usually train only twice a week. Just diving, it would take you a long time to acquire enough skill to get to the more elite level where they will let you train five or ten times a week.

There are some similarities between diving and trampolining, but also major differences. When you are doing a tramp routine, you don't do any blind tricks – that is, you always position yourself so you can see the trampoline bed and therefore where you are going. For instance, on the trampoline, you would never do a front somersault, as you would in diving, because coming over the top you simply can't see where the trampoline is.

My biggest trouble was when I was learning backward rotating dives. In trampolining, with backward rotating manoeuvres, you do a full twist or double twist and land feet-first. With diving, it's the opposite, and you hit the water head-first after a half, one and a half, or two and a half twist. Because I had learned in trampolining to finish any backward-rotating move by landing on my feet, stomach or back, obviously trying to avoid my head, I was having trouble adding the extra half-somersault in order to enter the water head-first. Every time I used my locked-in mental imagery from trampolining when doing my backward rotating dives, I would hit the water stomach- or back-first, as I would on the trampoline.

Performing both trampolining and diving in the one day, glitches were inevitable. Sometimes in the intensity of it all I forgot where I was and what I was doing. When I found myself landing on the trampoline head-first instead of on my feet, risking serious injury, I knew that keeping the two disciplines separate was easier said than done.

K.R. taught me a lot of good form that I then used in my trampolining. And I brought some techniques from trampolining into diving because I thought they looked better as well. When I was doing a mid-air twist, I didn't want to change the arm position that I'd learned in trampolining, as it came naturally to me and I was already a good twister. That position was acceptable in diving – it just wasn't traditional. Also from trampolining, I kept my back very flat instead of slightly arching it when I was doing a straight dive, because I thought it looked better. K.R. never told me to arch more; I think he was quite happy with the fact that I could keep a dead-straight position. And when I began to compete, I would get feedback from judges and other people saying that aesthetically it looked better dead straight. In fact, anything more than the slightest arch now looks really old-fashioned, and judges start taking marks off.

The judges have some fixed criteria and if you fail to meet them, you can lose points – for instance, the feet must always be pointed; and in the pike position, you need to keep your knees tight to your chest. But apart from basic things like that, diving can be a fairly creative sport, as it's mainly up to what the coach and judges think looks best. If a dive as a whole looks excellent and there is nothing fundamentally wrong with the diver's technique, then the judges are allowed to use their own judgment in scoring the dive. Some divers have their own unique style – sometimes that gets rewarded, and sometimes the judges don't like it so much. It's up to the diver and their coach to change the style if the judges don't like it, or keep perfecting it if it does work.

The next Trampoline World Age Games were in July 2001 in Odense, Denmark, which was grey and cold and seemed pretty lacklustre in comparison with Africa. I didn't know much about Denmark, and nothing about Odense, so had no clue what to do there away from competition, and, besides, I didn't have Grandma or Mum with me so I was under strict supervision. The most exciting thing I did was go across the road to the local corner store. I love licorice, but because I didn't have any money, I loitered inconspicuously around the pick'n'mix stand until the cashier turned his back. When he did so, I grabbed two bits of licorice, shoved them in my mouth, and spat them right back out again. I learnt that Danish licorice is really salty, and I learnt my lesson for stealing.

I competed in the 13-14 age group double-mini event in Odense. I was 13 and the boys I was competing against, even though they were the same age as me, were man-children. They had huge muscles and stubble, and one had a massive bush of hair protruding from his armpits. These big guys were so intimidating to a little boy like me. I was in absolute awe and felt inadequate in their company.

I didn't think I had a chance of beating them, and that knowledge relaxed my nerves and enabled me to go quietly about my passes. (In double-mini, each run-up and sequence of two tricks off the tramps is known as a 'pass'.) In an echo of a more famous victory I would have in a more high-profile sport on a far bigger stage seven years later, my main rivals fluffed some passes while I completed four solid passes, and at the end I had the points and they didn't. I was the world champion. When I saw my name on the winners' board I jumped 20 feet into the air and squealed like a little girl. Then I cried with joy. It was such a shock. I had beaten 55 rivals to take the world title, and in doing so I continued the success of fellow Wynnum PCYC trampoline champions Ji Wallace and Robyn Forbes. Melanie Tonks is obviously one hell of a coach. As I came off the floor of the Super Dome, the whole Australian team formed a tunnel for me to walk through. They were all cheering me. I felt so special. So did this count as being best in the world at something? Not to me it didn't.

In 2002 at the Australian Trampoline Nationals I won gold in the 13-14 years double-mini trampoline event, silver in the 13-14 years tumbling and the 13-17 years double-mini trampoline, and I placed third in the 13-17 years men's trampoline. I was named 2001 Junior Athlete of the Year at the Trampoline Nationals award dinner.

I had found something that I was very good at, but with all that relentless training — more than 30 hours a week — and going to school as well, I was exhausted physically and mentally. I couldn't go on this way. I had to choose one sport and let the other go. I had overestimated my ability to compartmentalise myself. The increasingly heavy demands of trying to be the best in both sports was doing my head and body in.

It was an agonising decision to make. In diving, after a year in the AIS's Talent Identification Squad, I had moved into the Queensland Elite Diving Team and was being trained by another Chinese coach, Chen Wen. My trampolining was going well enough for me to be a new force internationally; and I knew that the aerial awareness I'd gained from it helped my diving, just as the precise form drummed into me by the Chinese diving coaches had helped my trampoline form. But it was trampolining that I quit, with enormous reluctance.

Why did I choose to quit trampolining? Simply because I realised that I would have more chance of competing at an Olympics as a diver. Diving was an official Olympic sport, while at the Sydney 2000 games trampolining was an exhibition sport with no official funding. Therefore, only one place was available for each event on the Olympic team, and I'd be up against older and more experienced trampolinists to get one. I told myself that diving would be my ticket to being the best in the world, and win me medals, fame, friends and fans.

In the weeks when I was weighing up my decision, I told my trampoline coach Melanie Tonks that I was seriously considering giving tramp away. To her credit, she said she would hate to lose me but possibly it was a good idea because I could go further in diving than trampolining. She was giving me her blessing to dive. Before we parted, Melanie made me promise to consider a return to trampolining after I retired from diving and to give her the chance to take me to an Olympic Games. I said I would. I don't think either of us believed that. Trampolining is not a sport you can waft in and out of. Over the next months I eased down my trampoline training and then dropped out altogether.

I'm sure my doing one sport instead of two was a relief to my mum, grandma and grandad, financially at least. Battlers all, they had stretched their budget to fund my many trips away. No matter whether it was trampolining or diving, each overseas event cost around $5000. They also drove me from home to pool to school and back to pool and then to trampolining and home again for day after day, year after year.

After a few years of hard slog, six hours a day, six days a week, I started getting good results, and can fairly say I was one of the best junior divers in Australia. At the National Diving Championships in Adelaide in March and April 2002, I won the 14-15 years 1 metre, 3 metre and 10 metre platform events and came second in the synchronised diving event with New Zealand diver Tony Donaldson. We did a pretty good job of getting off the boards and into the water at the same time, considering we'd never even met before and we just did it for fun.

From those Nationals, I qualified for my first FINA World Junior Diving Championships in Aachen, Germany. The disappointment for me at that meet was that I failed my handstand dive off the 7.5 metre platform. (Divers under 16 don't compete in 10 metre yet.) I'd never learned how to do handstands as a trampolinist, so my diving coach had to teach me to do handstands on land first, then on the side of the pool, until I graduated to doing them from the 3 metre, 5 metre, 7.5 metre and finally 10 metre platform. Obviously I hadn't quite mastered the skill yet and hadn't yet developed all the upper-body strength I needed – not to mention that I was also pretty nervous. I got to the edge of the platform and kicked up for the handstand, but I couldn't hold it and came back down to my feet. And I did that twice. If you do it once, each judge takes off two points; but if you do it twice, it's an automatic fail. So I got zeros for the dive, and I got in so much trouble from my coach, Chen. I would continue to have problems with handstands for years.

At the 2001–2002 Brisbane Junior Sports Awards, I received the Encouragement Award, for athletes aged under 14. On the awards night, a reporter asked me my ultimate aim, and I replied that I dreamed of diving for Australia in the 2004 Athens Olympics, although I confessed that I thought I was still too young to be truly competitive. Swimmer Leisel Jones, who won a silver medal in the 100 metre breaststroke at the 2000 Sydney Olympic Games when she was 15 and two months, overheard me and piped up, 'Matthew, never say you're too young to represent in the Olympics. If you're good enough, you're old enough'.

★

In my first diving years, the sport was never as enjoyable for me as trampolining had been. Diving is fastidiously regimented and hitting the water again and again from 10 metres up hurts and batters your body. Coming off a 10 metre platform, you hit the surface of the water at 60 kilometres an hour, and at that velocity it feels like concrete. The brunt of breaking the initial surface tension is all taken by your wrists, and then once your wrists break the water, you just slip through the hole that you created for yourself. When I began training more on the 10 metre platform, my wrists started swelling up. They ached, and it looked like I had a half a tennis ball bulging out of each wrist. If I spent too long in training doing handstand dives off the platform or held a handstand for too long, as soon as I entered the water I would experience the most intense sharp pain in my wrist, to the point where I sometimes had to stop training. Then it would continue to ache and throb, and it would take a few days to settle down again.

Scans revealed several ganglion cysts and inflammation. I got cortisone injections, and I had to start taping my wrists to take some of the pressure off the joints. Ever since I was about 14 years old, I've had to tape my wrists every single time I get in the water, even if I'm just diving off the 1 metre springboard. I also changed my hand position as I go through the water. Now I grab the fingers of the leading hand and bend them backwards from the knuckles, rather than grabbing the back of the palm of the leading hand and bending the wrist backwards. I had to do this because I was no longer (and am still no longer) able to bend at the wrist due to the pain.

Platform divers tend to be susceptible to wrist ganglions and other injuries of the upper body: upper back and neck problems and shoulder problems such as dislocations, and torn rotator cuffs and triceps. Springboard divers tend to be more prone to lower-body injuries, developing problems with their knees, hips and lower backs. Stress fractures are common across the whole sport, perhaps because divers train intensely during the teenage years, when their bodies are still growing. That's when most back stress fractures happen to divers.

Because discipline, sacrifice and the ability to ignore pain are part and parcel of diving, many diving coaches feel that they have to be tyrants. Like my mother, I have never responded well to being yelled at or screamed at or ordered about, so whenever I came across a stern and demanding coach, as I inevitably did, we invariably clashed. There were elements of diving I enjoyed, definitely, but I missed trampolining's folksy community spirit, kind and caring officials and competitors – I missed its heart and soul.

Until I met my current coach, Chava Sobrino, for the seven years I was a member of the Australian Institute of Sport Diving Program I only ever had Chinese coaches who were ferociously dedicated and ruthless. These guys took no prisoners. Their manner was always curt, as if to show empathy would be a sign of weakness. And they seemed to treat divers as machines.

I believe that because there are so many athletes in China, the powers that be feel they can afford to treat them like machines because they know if one athlete breaks there is another just as good ready to step up and take his or her place. It's survival of the fittest. Only the strongest, and those prepared to put up with the demands on their body and spirit, survive in that system. In Australia, we don't have the numbers to choose from that they do in China, nor, generally, do our athletes have such a compliant attitude. While many Australian divers are happy to submit to the regimen, others are a little more like me in that they are prepared to push themselves to unbelievable lengths and make sacrifices to succeed, but see sport as one aspect of a greater, wider life, and try to wear a smile, maintain their self-respect and refuse to abase themselves before any coach.

I was then, as I am today, a free spirit (thanks again, Mum!), and I rebelled. I soon found myself the bad boy of the squad. I was unhappy, and that unhappiness manifested itself in injuries. There was never a time in those years when, as well as a chip on my shoulder, I wasn't carrying an injury, be it stress fractures in my back, muscle and joint pains, or ganglions in both wrists.

In 2002, at the age of 14, I had reached the required level of proficiency and graduated to the main AIS diving program. My coach was the renowned Hui Tong, who was the AIS national head coach, so Hui was probably not the ideal fellow to fall out with, as I quickly did.

Born in China in 1963, Hui had all the credentials. He was a champion gymnast before turning to diving. He represented his country from 1978 to 1989 and was proclaimed China's best diver from 1985 to 1989. In 1985 and 1987 he dived for China in the 10 metre event in the World Cup and won, and in the 1984 Olympics he was placed fourth. He coached the Canadian diving team before coming to Australia to be national head coach. You can't argue with Hui's results. He was the Australian team's head coach at the 2004 Athens Olympics, when Chantelle Newbery won gold in the women's 10 metre event and Loudy Tourky took the bronze, and in the men's 10 metre Mathew Helm won silver individually and bronze in the 10 metre synchro with Robert Newbery, Chantelle's husband. Under Hui's stern and dedicated leadership, Australia fought its way up to be the second best diving nation in the world, behind China.

Hui and I butted heads from the start. I just could not get along with him. I had low self-esteem anyway, and I bridled at the brusque way he laid down the law to me, the way he treated me like a naughty child. To be fair, he shouted at me rarely – mainly he just carped away at me. 'You're doing this wrong – why don't you listen?' He would tell me how he wanted me to dive, but then he never gave me affirmation or positive feedback about anything I did right. He only ever told me what I did wrong, and criticised my diving and me. Because I was hyper-sensitive, I twisted any criticism from anyone into a personal attack. This meant that his words made me feel worthless and hopeless. I was filled with angst. On top of having to remember the sequences of movements in my dives, I was also constantly worrying about whether I was doing them all the right way. Was there a better way? Was I even thinking the right way? What if I was psychologically sabotaging myself by thinking the wrong way? I felt I had nobody to talk to who could understand the turmoil I was in.

I came to despise diving. I obsessed that I had made a terrible mistake in sacrificing trampolining, a sport which I had loved and was good at, and the freedom and fun of youth for Hui and his diving program. In my unhappy frame of mind, joining the diving squad each day was like voluntarily going to jail and doing hard labour. I felt trapped training for so long each day for a sport I wasn't enjoying.

Criticism was an arrow to my heart. Some people are motivated by being told they are no good. Not me. I respond to encouragement. My mindset had always been that I had to be perfect so people would like me. According to Hui –

at least according to *my interpretation* of his words and actions towards me – I was imperfection personified. I interpreted the way in which he treated me as his way of telling me that I wasn't good enough and I never would be, and that I was wasting his time. Of course, he never said that, but that's all I could hear.

I didn't handle things well. I fought back at Hui by being passively aggressive: I was stubborn, continuing to dive the way I wanted rather than the way he wanted me to, and giving him the scowling silent treatment when he criticised me. I was just so angry.

Normally, once you've done a dive, you get some feedback from your coach at the side of the pool and then pick up the most essential diving tool – your chamois – from the pool deck and walk back up the stairs to the board or platform to dry yourself. If you don't dry off, you get cold while you wait your turn. When you're wet, there is more of a risk your hands will slip off your legs and you'll make a complete shemozzle of your dive. And a drop of water might flick in your eye and completely disorientate you. Once it's your turn, you throw your chamois back down onto the pool deck and dive again.

But to get my daily training program over quickly and make my escape, I rushed through my program, doing a dive, leaping out of the pool and running all the way up the stairs to the board to dive again. I wouldn't even dry myself. People thought I was crazy. God knows what Hui thought of me. Actually I *do* know. He must have thought I was a pest and a pain, and he had every reason to.

Depending on which springboard or platform I was diving from, I could be doing anywhere from about forty-five to sixty dives in one training session. In Brisbane our afternoon sessions were three and a half hours long. Because I rushed between my dives, I would finish my set training program after two and a half hours. Then I would be made to do more, to get me through the extra hour. The whole reason I trained so quickly was to get out of that pool as soon as possible because I hated being there, but then I had to do more dives than everybody else just because I trained harder and faster – and that made me even more resentful.

I realise now that I was just too intimidated to approach Hui and request, person to person, that we try to iron out our huge differences, so I kept up my passive resistance. Even if I had summoned the courage to have it out with Hui, I don't think I would have been able to communicate my feelings to him in a way that would have been productive. My pent-up anger and frustration may have made me lose my temper, which would have only made things worse. I tried to bottle up my feelings and stick it out, because there were moments I knew that I could dive better than I could do anything else in the world, and I was better off diving with Hui than not diving at all.

To try to make things better, I had regular sessions with a sports psychologist. I was not the only one of Hui's divers who resorted to counselling to try to learn how to communicate with him. The psychologist told me, as she had told other divers who'd butted heads with Hui, that he was the coach and a fine one at that; in her view, he would never change, and it was up to *me* to change. He was the coach and I was the athlete, and it was up to me to alter my ways so that he would approve of me. I should swallow my pride and humour him, and if I was unable to genuinely adjust my attitude, I should simply pretend to and reap the benefits of his coaching. If I couldn't do that, there was nothing for me to do but quit.

Today I know that it wasn't his fault that our relationship was so dysfunctional. I didn't then, when I was so young, but today I accept the blame. As a coach, Hui was merely doing, in the best way he knew, what he had always done and what he was being paid by the AIS to do. He was treating me in a way that he believed would help me to win Olympic medals. Obviously, many of the other Aussies at the AIS were happy to follow Hui's dictates, and have successful careers to show for it. Our problem was me. In my mind, I blew the problem out of proportion; I just couldn't cope with a hard-arse.

4

the black dog
(matt's best friend)

Hui maintained his pressure on me. He obviously thought my results were testimony to his tough coaching, and he was no doubt right. I continued to bite my lip and put up with what I interpreted as his barbs and nagging, but repressing my feelings took a toll. I was growing sadder and sadder, angrier and angrier. Today I understand that what was happening to me at this stage of my life was my burgeoning depression, for this is what the sadness and tears had always been.

I realise now that I suffer from clinical depression, like my mum, and that depression caused my black moods and low self-esteem as a child and, consequently, my desperate need to be admired by others. Before doctors and psychologists told me this, I blamed diving alone for bringing me down. I blamed diving and Hui for my lack of any social life.

I blamed diving for all the shit that was weighing me down. *Everything* was its fault.

Then again, and here is the terrible anomaly, diving was my only ticket to being special. I was doing very well at diving, representing at state and national level, but my self-esteem was so rock-bottom that I was incapable of appreciating what I was achieving.

I had a best friend, a girl. I had known her since she had joined my group in the Talent Identification Squad, training with K.R. Back when I had moved up to the Queensland Elite Diving Team, she actually went straight into the AIS squad, because they thought she had such potential. She had quit diving for a time, as she'd had anorexia, but she had now returned to the AIS squad. She was the first person to truly give me the time of day, to actually be interested in me and in having a friendship with me. We were together every chance we got, and because she lived near me, we could carpool to training and have weekend sleepovers at her house. She and I were soul mates and could talk about anything. After having no real friends in primary school, it felt wonderful to have this one intense platonic friendship and to know that somebody actually 'got' me. I was happy to go along with the intensity of it: it was something new for me, and I didn't want it to go away.

My friend was also depressed, and her depression manifested in self-harm. She cut her wrists, where it could be hidden by strapping tape. She explained to me that inflicting pain on herself eased her despair. Then one day my friend made a serious attempt to kill herself. She failed, thank God.

While she was recovering in hospital, I called her to give her my love, and she was cold to me. I had never heard her sound like this. She told me she never wanted to talk to me again. I was beside myself and had no clue why she was freezing me out. Today I do. Soon after her suicide attempt, my friend wrote me a letter saying that she was so sad that her only way out was to die. I had hidden the letter in what I thought was a safe place, inside one of my encylopedias. My mum found it and gave it to the girl's father. When her dad confronted her, my friend concluded that I had passed the letter to Mum and so betrayed her trust. I was shattered. I wanted to die too. I drank half a bottle of Painstop, hoping that would be enough to kill myself. I was no more successful at suicide than my friend had been. I slept from 3pm that afternoon until 7 the next morning then woke up groggy but quite OK.

At this point I began cutting myself. Self-harm was, I suppose, a warped tribute to my depressed friend. She believed cutting herself eased her pain. Perhaps, I hoped, slicing into myself with a sharp object would ease mine.

I believe that cutting myself, summoning the courage to sink the blade into my skin and feeling the sting and waiting for the blood to rise and gush, was a cry for someone to help me end my sadness and anger. It was also a way to inflict upon myself the pain I felt I deserved because I considered myself to be such a miserable creature. I had a problem and I cut myself and bled and, symbolically, the problem I'd been faced with had been exorcised by my razor blade. That's one problem I didn't have any more. That's how I rationalised it when I was hacking at my arms. Of course I was fooling myself. I laid my flesh open, the wounds healed, my problem remained.

I thought I was escaping my demons, but I was not; I was compounding them. That's why my depression would go on for so long and get so bad. I never figured out an acceptable way of dealing with my pain and anger.

I did regularly talk to the sports psychologist about my depression, but I found cutting myself more helpful. It's not that she wasn't compassionate, but sports psychologists are really there to get the best performance out of athletes. And I think I may have downplayed the seriousness of my depression as well, because I felt quite a lot of shame about being depressed. I saw it as a weakness, and part of the mentality of elite sport is that you don't want to be seen as being weak.

My first big cutting episode was when I was aged 14, at a junior national diving competition. I was furious with Hui over something critical that he said to me, and I lashed out at him by lashing out at myself. I was in the shower and there in the stall was a Gillette safety razor. As the water coursed down on me from the shower head, I cracked the razor apart with a can of Lynx deodorant and took out the blade and swung, literally swung, at my arm with it, making cross hatch cuts up and down my arm. I was in a frenzy and don't remember it hurting while I was doing it. I lost a fair amount of blood down that sink-hole. It reminded me of the shower scene in *Psycho*. Finally I stopped slashing myself and turned off the shower. I bound the wounds with strapping tape. Later Hui asked me why my arm was bandaged and I told him that I had corked the muscle in my arm and had had to strap it. He accepted my explanation. I spent the next weeks wearing long sleeved shirts to cover up the scars.

It would turn out that I couldn't hide those scars forever, and I would go on to have another two major cutting episodes that I would not be able to cover up either. But I also had numerous smaller episodes that I could hide easily. I became addicted to cutting; it was my first port of call. Whenever something was going wrong in my life or whenever I just couldn't handle a feeling, it was the first thing I resorted to.

My depression sent me on a desperate search for happiness in my life, and I ran off the rails. I began going to gay nightclubs at age 14. Yes, I was four years under-age. My athletic physique and facial features made me look older than 14, but not 18. However, Brisbane's licensing laws were not enforced very strictly then, and as often as not, I brazenly breezed by the doormen at my favourite Fortitude Valley clubs without a question being asked. Just in case, I kept a fake ID handy, or sometimes I borrowed the ID of a friend who resembled me. I was only caught out once, when I was 17, and the friend whose ID I'd borrowed was fined and Mum reimbursed him. One establishment where I enjoyed the red carpet treatment was a Valley club run by a man who fancied me. I'd say to the bouncer, 'So-and-so and I, we're good mates,' and in I'd go, welcomed like a VIP.

I had known since I was very young that I was gay. But I'd also understood that much of society – certainly the section of society where I existed – and the nuns at my school, in particular, frowned on homosexuality and persecuted those who practised it, so until I was 11, I wore a rubber band around my wrist and flicked it every time I had a gay thought. This was an attempt at conditioning myself to stop being gay and to do what society demanded and embrace heterosexuality. Of course, suppressing my natural instincts led to more bad than good, as I was racked by guilt and repressed desire.

I often wonder if my growing realisation that I was gay played a part, even unconsciously, in my depression. I don't think so. I never had a real problem with being gay. But knowing that being straight is the default sexuality in our society, because heterosexual relationships are the foundation of marriage and parenthood, and that gay men and women are often discriminated against, I did wonder for a bit if I could save myself all this strife and change my sexuality. I dated girls in my trampoline squad when I was 12 and 13, and that was fun; and then when I was a little older I slept with girls, and that was pretty good, too. I had sex with girls pretty much through my teenage years and I enjoyed it. It wasn't until I was 18, when I fell in love, that I accepted once and for all that I was gay by nature and preference. Anyone close to me had known for yonks. Some people had their suspicions, which I didn't bother to dispel.

With only a few exceptions, in the AIS Diving Program, I didn't get along with the male athletes with whom I trained. I suspected that this was because they could see I was gay and were uncomfortable with that. Some of those boys were pretty unpleasant, and I convinced myself that they would be vicious to me had they known for sure, so, as they say, I neither confirmed nor denied. In reality, rather than in the tortured daydreams I had back then, they may have been absolutely fine with me being gay. What may have made them uncomfortable was that I was not forthright about it. I have no idea how Hui would have reacted if I'd come out at Chandler, but I suspected not too favourably.

At school, I'm sure the kids had worked out that I was gay, because I was such an exhibitionist, and there was the little matter of my pretty leotards. Occasionally if a classmate put the question to me, as kids are prone to do, I might say I was bi. At one of the trampoline nationals, I had a sexual experience with a boy who also went to my school. He returned to class and told people what had happened, and of course soon the scandal was all over the playground. I denied it for a while but eventually I just began to accept it. I started admitting I was gay, because, I reasoned, if you say, 'Yes, I am a fag, what's the big deal?' then it'll deprive the finger pointers of their fun. It's no fun calling a fag a fag when he happily calls himself one. So at school I didn't get teased about being gay from Year 10 onwards.

I had not long turned 15 when I cut myself again. It happened after a row with Mum. By wearing long sleeves, I had concealed from her my scarred arm from the earlier cutting, but one day she chanced to see the latticework of scars. She demanded to know what had happened. I told her what I'd done. She lost her temper. We'd had many, many fights in recent times – typically we'd squabble about something petty, and then she'd remember some past issue and she'd bring that up and the whole row would snowball – but this was by far our biggest blow-up. There was serious screaming, she at me and me at her. She kicked me out of our home. I went to Grandma, who was, as ever, glad to have me to stay with her. What I did next was no way to repay my grandma's kindness. All I wanted to do was hit back at Mum. I went to Grandma's bathroom, stood under the shower and started swinging another blade I'd extracted from a safety razor, inflicting more than 40 superficial cuts in a row on my left forearm. Next day, Grandma – God knows what she thought she had taken on by bringing me into her home – took me to a GP, who treated my wounds and diagnosed depression and generalised anxiety disorder with panic attacks. I had always used my high anxiety to rev up my adrenaline for competing. That's functional stress – but my anxiety had become dysfunctional.

Some people have internalised panic attacks, which happen mostly inside the person's own mind and might not even be all that apparent to others, but mine were very externalised. I would cry and crouch down, curled up in the foetal position. My heart would pound and I would feel as though I was going to die. I would hyperventilate so much that my face went tingly from pins and needles and my hands started cramping. I've had about eight major panic attacks like that in total in my life since I was about 15.

Aside from the panic attacks, I was always on edge, with this sense of dread hanging over me. I would turn everyday mundane things into a cause for anxiety. I would blow things out of proportion to the point where, say I was running late, it would seem like a big catastrophe, as if it were the end of the world and I was going to be in *so* much trouble – much more trouble than I would be in reality (except in the case of training, as I would get into trouble then).

I had trouble sleeping, too. There were nights when I would move my pillow and try sleeping with my head at the other end of my bed, or I would try sleeping on the floor. Other nights, I would push the bed slightly away from the wall and sleep in the gap, because I felt more secure and protected wedged there. And as a teenager I always slept in a sleeping bag; I really liked the feeling of being safely wrapped up, cocooned. I put the sleeping bag on top of my bed or out on the veranda when it was really hot.

Another indication of my anxiety was that I continually bit my nails and pulled off the quicks and the skin around the nails. I'd been doing that ever since I was about 5 years old, and now I was older I had started pulling my beard hairs out, too. There is actually a word for this compulsion, trichotillomania.

As well as being worried about everyday things like being late, I had a more existential sort of anxiety. I worried about whether my mind was just going to slip away and I would be gone forever, stuck in a black purgatory. So I would jiggle my legs when I was sitting, bouncing them up and down as a way of keeping myself psychologically present, like a continual reminder that I exist, that I'm here, that I'm alive.

Even now I still bite my nails and pull at the skin around them, and my legs are always bouncing. I'd had these tendencies ever since I was little; I think it came from tensing up all the time because I didn't know if I had done something to deserve a smack or being yelled at by Mum.

The doctor prescribed for me an antidepressant and anti-anxiety drug. Knowing nothing about antidepressants, I assumed the drug would not just blunt my feelings of despair but actually make me happy. It in fact took the edge off *all* my emotions. I didn't feel as sad as before. The best way I can describe it is that it seemed as if my life was in monochrome. I took the drug for a year or so, then, hating not feeling *anything*, I took myself off it. I plunged straight back into a dark depression. I felt sad and angry all the time.

My usual response to Hui's criticism was to be passive aggressive, turning my anger upon myself. Now, after the terrible argument with Mum and the need I felt to self-harm, I feared I was losing all self-control and would become actively aggressive with Hui, as I had been with Mum. I was so pissed off with him for making me do something – diving – that I despised. I didn't want to be seen to be an angry person like that. So I internalised my rage and let it seethe. I was becoming a very disturbed young man.

The third major time I cut myself I was at a party. I was 16. For once I didn't do it as a response to the problems in my life. I did it because on this particular night I was being a dickhead show-off. There were some emos at this party, kids with black clothes and dyed black hair, white skin and a cynical slacker attitude, who were saying how cool it was to self-harm. They all came with their blades, which they produced and began to slowly draw lightly across their inner arms, causing tiny scratches. I decided to show these wimps how self-harm was really done. Making sure they were all watching, I took a razor blade and swung at my arm to get a nice deep cut. The thick blade laid my forearm wide open. The cut was 7 centimetres long and 3 centimetres wide and so deep it exposed the sinews. My display had the desired effect. The emos were horrified. Some turned even whiter than normal. A couple gagged. I was in total shock and felt no pain. After I'd cut my arm, it took a while for the blood to well and then gush over everything. The girl who was hosting the party ran to grab a big Elastoplast bandage roll, and she wrapped it around and around my arm. I called my grandma to collect me, and she rushed me to the Mater Hospital.

It took the nurse ages to unwrap the blood-soaked bandages. Then she inserted eight stitches in my arm, and as she sewed me back together, she admonished me like I was a naughty child. 'Why did you do such a silly thing? Now that wasn't a sensible thing to do, was it?' I felt so degraded.

Understandably, Grandma was worried sick about me. Fearing I would self-harm again, she went around the house hiding anything I could use to cut myself. Blades, paint scrapers, pencils with that sharp metal bit on the end that holds the rubber – all got stashed away.

At the pool, I asked my diving coaches if I could have a little time off diving so I wouldn't wet or break my stitches when I hit the water – of course I didn't tell them how I came by my wounds – and one person snapped at me, 'We're an institute of excellence, not a welfare service'.

I stopped cutting myself after that episode. I felt so ashamed and guilty for putting Grandma through another terrible experience. I also realised, perhaps in the nick of time, that self-harm was not an acceptable way to deal with my emotions. I could have died. I didn't want to die. I also knew I was being cruel to Grandma, and she didn't deserve that.

I found other ways to take the edge off my unhappiness. By now I was a regular at the gay clubs of Fortitude Valley on weekends and occasionally during the week. I needed to escape diving and Hui, and the sadness and anger that was poisoning me.

I threw myself into the excitement, the danger, the thumping music, the drinking. I made friends quickly, and

I met boys. I danced till daylight. I didn't realise at first that most of the others who were dancing with me at 5am were on ecstasy and speed. I thought everyone had as much natural energy as me. So many people offered me drugs, and before too long I was doing drugs too. I smoked pot regularly and dipped into other drugs. I tried LSD when I was 16, maybe 17. I was in a club, and next day I had no memory of big patches of that night. That didn't stop me taking LSD again.

I never felt remorseful after a big night when I awoke with a hangover and no memory. After years in a diving straitjacket, partying was a thrill. In clubs, I felt comfortable. The boy who had always wanted people to like him and tied himself in knots trying to ingratiate himself with others, was finally pleasing himself.

I often wonder today if any of those people whom I partied with way back then recognised me on the Olympic dais in 2008 and wondered, 'Surely that's not the Matt Mitcham I knew. Olympic Gold – how the hell did that happen?'

Because the only time I felt happy was when I was dancing for hours on end in clubs, I came to associate drugs and clubbing with happiness, so it's no surprise that I became addicted to those things. I was only able to endure the horrible diving, schoolwork, go-to-bed-early weekdays because I knew the weekend with its clubs and sex and drugs and dancing and fun was on its way. I couldn't wait for Friday night, Saturday and Sunday to roll around. The weekend was the only time when I was truly happy and didn't have to do the things I hated. I liked to wring the most out of my weekend, and would stay out until 5 on Monday morning, go across the road from the nightclub to munch on a sausage roll for breakfast, then drive out to Chandler for 6am training. The comedown from the weekend on Tuesdays and Wednesdays was awful. There was an even blacker cloud hanging over me, waiting to descend and engulf me. Clubbing made it go away. Training and school brought it back. By Thursday morning I was counting the minutes till Friday night.

I must make it perfectly clear right now that the drugs I took were never performance-enhancing drugs – they were recreational narcotics. I knew how long the drugs remained in my system and timed my use of them according to when I would be likely to be drug-tested at diving events.

I also became a binge drinker. Every weekend I drank to annihilate myself. I drank to get smashed, throw up and fall unconscious. I poured whatever was handy – usually spirits – down my throat. I sculled bourbon straight from the bottle. I took drugs and got drunk to escape to another place, away from the pressure and the sadness.

It will come as no surprise that I was not exactly a model student at Mansfield High. I rarely did homework, and the reason was I was never home. I was either diving or partying. I was sneaking out a lot at night; I'd creep back into Grandma's at 3.30 in the morning, have 90 minutes' sleep, then get up and go to diving. I'm still not sure how I pulled it off. My grades in maths and English, subjects I wasn't too interested in, were awful. In French, which I loved, I did well. Mansfield High had a French Immersion course in which Year 8-10 students could study mathematics, science, history, geography and French completely in French. I had done a little French in primary school and loved the language and had a knack for it. The challenge appealed to me.

After spending all day in French mode, immersing myself in it and tackling my subjects in the language, when I went home to my grandma's I thought and spoke in French. Having no French herself, my grandma would have to remind me that if I wanted her to understand what I was saying I would need to stick to English.

Because I was still at school and living at Grandma's after Mum had shown me the door, I qualified for $300 a week Centrelink payments. That was how I paid board to my grandmother and for any other expenses.

My poor long-suffering Grandma. I will never be able to atone for what I did to her. I was no longer cutting myself but I was still self-harming with booze and drugs. Grandma realised that I was sneaking out and partying because she opened up one of my bank statements that arrived in the mail and saw that I'd been making regular withdrawals at nightclub ATM machines at 2 or 3 in the morning. It was nothing for me to spend $50 or $100 a night on alcohol. My grandmother banned me from going out, but I waited until she was asleep to escape to wherever the fun was.

From my bedroom I couldn't jump out of the window to the yard because directly below was a big concrete slab with metal rods sticking out of it. So I would leave my bedroom from a door leading onto the veranda and slide down a pole into the yard. Soon Grandma realised what I was up to and locked the door in my bedroom. Ever-resourceful, I exited the kitchen door onto the veranda and got out that way. She soon tumbled to my ploy and locked that door and hid the key. I climbed out my bedroom and the kitchen windows and she locked them. That meant I had to negotiate the stairs, many of which creaked when I stepped on them. I learned which ones held my weight without betraying me. Grandma soon got wise to that, and she ended up locking every door and window in that house. There was no way out. I put that poor lady through so much. She must love me very much to have endured what she did.

5

retirement is for old folks

My form remained good enough to fool Hui. If he knew how I was knocking myself around he would have expelled me from the team immediately and without a qualm. In 2004, at the Australian Open Championships in Hobart, I teamed with Gene Kimlin to win silver in the 3 metre and the 10 metre synchro events, placed third in the 10 metre platform event, and finished third in the 1 metre and fourth in the 3 metre events. At the Olympic trials mid-year, I came third in the 3 metre and 10 metre individual events and second in 10 metre and 3 metre synchro, which meant I missed out on going to the Athens Games by one spot in all four disciplines.

In October of 2004, I represented Australia in the World Junior Championships in Belem, Brazil, and I won silver medals in the 1 metre and 10 metre individual events and 3 metre synchro with Scott Robertson. Just before the 3 metre individual final, one of the Australian boys, a kid who picked on me at training in Brisbane, said something to me that really upset me, so I went off into a field behind the pool and sat there trying to pull myself together. The more I tried to settle myself down, the more panic-stricken I became; I began hyperventilating, shaking and weeping, and my hands started cramping up. I told myself I was overreacting to a stupid comment, and eventually got myself back under control. I stood up and returned to the pool for my event. All it took was an encounter with the very caring Australian massage therapist, who could see I was upset and tried to comfort me, and I fell in a heap again, crying uncontrollably. He recognised that I was having a panic attack and talked me through it until it subsided. A group of Russian girl divers witnessed the whole grisly scene. Before then, I had caught them ogling me. After seeing me fall apart, all that stopped. I can't say I blame them. Oh, and I messed up in the final. I was so embarrassed, about the panic attack and not diving well. That night when I walked into the dinner hall, I thought everyone would be looking at me and judging me. I started having another panic attack, and I had to walk straight back out.

Articles about me started popping up, and Grandma cut every one out and stuck them in a scrapbook. In December

2004, Brisbane's *South-East Advertiser* newspaper profiled me after I won the McDonald's Quest Young Star Sports Award. 'This summer [Matthew is] proving he has the dedication of an elite sportsman,' the story said. It mentioned that I was planning to celebrate Christmas by taking a couple of days away from the pool. That reporter, in writing such a cheery and positive article, had no idea how bad things were right then between Hui and me, and how the periods of sadness and tears which I'd experienced from childhood were engulfing me.

In 2005, I improved on my form of the previous year. In January at the Australian Youth Olympic Festival in Sydney, I won silver in the 1 metre and gold in the 3 metre, 3 metre synchro (with Scott Robertson) and 10 metre. In the 10 metre, I scored 555.80, including several 9s and 9.5s, to beat Malaysian Bryan Nickson, who had competed at the Athens Olympics. My medal haul made me the festival's most successful athlete. And at the Australian Open Championships on the Gold Coast, I was placed first in the 1 metre, and second in the 3 metre and 3 metre synchro (with Gene Kimlin), and I was third in the 10 metre.

The only black spot in a successful year of diving was when I fell from a somersaulting box and hurt my back while doing somersaults with my synchro diving partner Robert Newbery in a warm-up session at the FINA World

Championships in Montreal, Canada. Unfortunately the event I was warming up for was the 10 metre synchro platform. I landed with the corner of the box smashing into the base of my spine. I screamed and hit the floor. I left the pool in the most dramatic of fashions, being wheeled out on a spine board. I was rushed to hospital for an x-ray, which proved I hadn't broken anything, but there was no way I could have dived. This was unfortunate for Robert who, unable to find anyone to team with at such short notice, was left unable to compete.

In 2005 I competed in the China Grand Prix event, and my bronze in the 3 metre event was my first open international medal.

I always enjoyed going to China because it's just so alien, such a different world. I would get the Chinese coaches in Brisbane to teach me little phrases here and there, like 'Thank you', 'Hello', 'How are you?', 'See you tomorrow', 'Too fat', 'Too slow', 'Stupid'. But when the Chinese coaches talked amongst each other, discussing the divers, I started picking up a few too many words for their liking, and they stopped teaching me Chinese. So in the summer holidays at the end of 2005 I did an intensive Mandarin course at Queensland University of Technology. Because I had already studied other languages, I absorbed it quickly and learned a surprising amount – enough that now when I compete in China I'm able to make jokes or figure out how to get from A to B, ask people their name and how old they are and what they do for a living, and tell people a bit about myself.

At 16, 17 and 18, I had a number of boyfriends and casual sexual partners. I had a rule that I never broke: Never go home with someone I'd just met at a club when I was vulnerable and danger-prone – that is, when my thinking was impaired by drinking or drugs or I had just got carried away with the partying. Bad things can happen in that world. I'd heard many stories from my friends of the predators who hang around clubs preying on boys, and I didn't want to put myself in a position where I was not in control. If I was attracted to someone then I would make sure that I waited until I liked and trusted him before we slept together.

One time when I did sleep with a virtual stranger, I came to regret it. I was at a bar with my then-best friend and my mother, and we were all boogeying. (Yes, my mum came to clubs with me. Nothing was going to stop me from going out, she figured, so it was better she was there with me at least.) Across the room, I noticed a guy, shaved head, muscles, mid-30s, making eyes at me. I was definitely attracted, and returned the compliment. Later we exchanged phone numbers. I asked him what he did for a living and he replied, 'I'm a cop'. I stiffened, then had a mini freak out. 'Shit ... shit ... shit ... I'm too pretty to go to jail,' I thought. The man smiled and said to relax. 'You're fine. I'm off-duty.' Sweet relief. He asked me how old I was and I told him 16. He said he had no problem with that and the following day we met and had sex, but it was awkward and unpleasant, and I never saw him again.

I was having way too much fun to be really interested in a steady relationship, although from time to time a sexual encounter would develop into a genuine friendship. A few of the people I met in those Fortitude Valley clubs are close to me today. Most of the others were club-goers as off their face as I probably was and I forgot them instantly. When the music is loud and you're dancing and you're ecstatic on ecstasy, everyone is your friend. Those I stay in contact with still cared about me in the cold light of day, when the drugs and euphoria had worn off.

I started taking ecstasy soon after I turned 18, in 2006. Till then it was only ever pot and LSD. I fell in love with ecstasy. To me, there was a reason they called it that. On a big night, I rationed myself to two and a half pills. That probably sounds like a lot but, believe me, to party animals it's nothing. I would have one tablet at the beginning of the party and swallow a half-tablet every couple of hours for the rest of the night and into the next day to maintain my high.

I was on an emotional rollercoaster in 2006. Diving was hard, and I hated the sport and my coaches more than ever, and

I reached out for pills like a drowning man grasps a lifebuoy. I was depressed and anxious, and school wasn't going well. I was so exhausted by my diving training and competing and my weekend partying that I often nodded off to sleep in class, to the hilarity of everyone. My marks were down. I didn't care. The only reason I was even *at* school was to qualify for living-away-from-home welfare payments. I repeated Year 12 so I'd be eligible for weekly handouts for another year.

At the Australian Open Championships in Melbourne early in the year, I won silver in the 3 metre and 3 metre synchro, with Scott once more, and third in the 10 metre. Then, in March, Melbourne hosted the 2006 Commonwealth Games, and I was selected to represent Australia in the 3 metre dive and the 3 metre synchro event, with Scott Robertson, as well as in the 1 metre and 10 metre events. I dived well, but not well enough. I placed fourth in the 3 metre and the 3 metre synchro, and fifth in the 1 metre and 10 metre events. I considered myself to be the biggest loser because I entered so many events and was one of the only divers on the Australian team who didn't win a medal. That was, and is, so typical of me. Many athletes would consider it an honour to even represent their country at such a huge and important event. Not me. As usual I found a reason to beat myself up.

In the Fort Lauderdale, Florida, leg of the FINA Grand Prix series, I dived with Scott in the 3 metre synchro and we took home bronze. In the Sydney and Zhuhai legs of the Grand Prix series, Scott and I came fourth in the 3 metre synchro.

I competed at the 2006 FINA Diving World Cup in Changshu that July. I didn't want to be there. I'd stopped seeing diving as my saviour. My diving career was unravelling anyway. Two incidents at those championships were the catalyst for me to quit the sport.

First, I had a huge falling out with the team manager. Looking back, we both behaved in a silly manner. I was getting changed to go to the march-on for my event, when the athletes are presented to the crowd, usually before a final. The divers dress in the full tracksuit uniforms of their countries and walk out onto the pool deck in the order in which they're going to compete, and the announcer says their name and what country they're from. I hadn't got around to putting on my sandshoes yet, and he said, 'I hope you're going to put shoes on,' assuming for some reason that I had been planning not to. I ignored him, and he grimaced and made a noise at me – 'Pffff' – to signal his disgust. I flared up. 'Don't pffff me.' He said, 'I'll pffff you if I choose to.' It was so infantile. I stormed off. That altercation put me in a bad mood for the entire event.

Then came the straw that broke this little camel's back. I was coming third in the final of the 10 metre platform event and I was confident I could secure a medal by nailing the last of my six dives, a new one in my repertoire, a back two and a half somersault with two and a half twist. This was the hardest dive anyone in the world was doing at that time (and the one that would win me Olympic gold in 2008). I was hyped up, edgy, bouncing manically on the balls of my feet as the time neared for my make-or-break dive. Hui, however, and quite rightly I understand now, told me to calm down and compose myself. I came right back at him, addressed him contemptuously as if he was not my exalted coach but a know-nothing idiot. 'I *need* to get pumped up to make this last dive.'

I continued to work myself up into a state, twitching and bouncing until it was my turn … and I overcooked the dive, rolling over onto my back as I hit the water. I placed fifth. As I emerged disconsolately from the water, Hui began yelling at me from across the pool, so loudly that everyone could hear. He yelled that because I'd defied him I'd lost the bronze medal. I stood there and endured his blast as other competitors looked away embarrassed for me. I felt so ashamed, so worthless.

The next day the team manager and Hui presented me with a letter. It said that my recent actions had put me in breach of the National Squad Performance Standards, specifically Section A: Standards and Commitment of National Squad Athletes; No.5, Respect for the Training

Environment. My defiant rudeness to Hui Tong had displayed a lack of respect for the head coach and constituted non-compliance with the coach's instructions. The letter was a warning that I was in violation of the Performance Standards and that a repeat offence would lead them to review my status in the squad.

Then Hui told me that as punishment for my insolence he was forbidding me to compete in the World Junior Championships in Malaysia the following month. I had been keenly looking forward to that event because I'd always had a lot of fun with the kids who competed there, and it would be my last World Juniors. I had won a number of silver medals at the previous Juniors meet in 2004, when I was 16, and felt confident that I'd come home this time with gold. Also, I was counting on taking a three-week holiday in Japan right afterwards. I felt I'd earned a break because I had been diving on the national, international junior, as well as the open circuit all year; no one had competed in as many events over the past 12 months as me. Now Hui told me that my holiday had been reduced from three weeks to two weeks and was starting immediately, and that right afterward he expected me to report for training. Obviously this sudden change of plan did not leave me sufficient time to organise and take my trip to Japan. So, in effect, Hui had banned me from the World Juniors and my Japanese vacation.

I had had enough. I booked a flight out of Shanghai to Brisbane leaving the very next day. On arrival in Brisbane, indulging a mad spur of the moment whim, I booked another flight, to Sydney.

I knew no one in that city. I had no idea where I was going to stay. I didn't have much money. What all this was about was doing something outrageous to get back at the diving set-up at Chandler; escaping to what I hoped would be the bright party lights of Sydney would be my revenge. At the accommodation desk at Sydney Airport I found a brochure for a backpackers' hostel in Forbes Street in the inner Sydney suburb of Darlinghurst and, because I couldn't afford cab fare, caught a shuttle bus to Darlinghurst and checked in. It was a miserable place, but it would have to do for now. Being too afraid to explore a big, strange city on my own, I jumped on the internet, and after much to-ing and fro-ing I contacted a friend of a friend and told him I was in town for a week and asked could he show me a few of his favourite clubs.

He agreed to meet me for a night out. I went to his place and, after one look at his wardrobe, I realised he was a drag queen. He was a fun guy. We messed about playing dress-ups and that was a hoot. I changed back into my street clothes to go out; he stayed in drag. We met one of his friends, who was also a drag queen, on the way to the club. I ended up staying with the friend for a week. We had a really good time partying and clubbing every night, and an extra bonus of sharing his bed was that I didn't have to spend a single night at the backpackers' hostel.

During the day, when he went to work, I would go for walks around the city, completely absent of purpose or destination. I had the luxury of coming and going from the flat as I liked, because he had graciously entrusted me with the spare key. Every evening when he returned, I had put a new desktop picture on his gigantic computer monitor, showcasing my favourite cross-dressing creation of the day. I couldn't help myself — his entire apartment was an enormous walk-in wardrobe.

All of his friends were drag queens, so after several days of gentle persuasion (the kind that drag queens are renowned for) I finally got over my immobilising self-consciousness and into the spirit of being on vacation … I took one of my characters out into the big, bad world.

Her name was Matilda Moneypenny. She had long, brown, curly locks, wore a sequinned Union Jack mini-dress à la Ginger Spice, and sported white, knee-high, vinyl 'eff me' boots. What a sight: dressed like a whore, with a swagger like a transvestite truck driver, strutting up Oxford Street at 10am on a school day, with 'Walk Like a Man' by The Four Seasons playing in my head as the soundtrack. Oddly enough, that's one of the very few times in my life that I haven't cared about what anyone thought of me — probably because I wasn't actually me.

The evening before I was due to fly home to Brisbane and resume diving with Hui — providing that he would have me, of course — I met the man who is my partner to this day.

I'd been clubbing in Darlinghurst; it was 5.30am and I was sitting at the bus stop outside the club. A man in his 30s approached. I was a little apprehensive because he looked higher than a kite. He plonked himself down next to me theatrically and said, 'Hey, see that guy over there; his name is Lachlan' — he pointed to a tall, attractive, obviously shy guy standing several metres away — 'and he's having a party at his place when the club closes. He wants you to come along'. I thought for a nanosecond, looked again at Lachlan, and replied, 'Why not'.

We all returned to the club together and danced some more. After the sun came up, we went to Lachlan's apartment in Potts Point for a recovery party where precious little recovering took place. We danced all day at Lachlan's until we literally dropped. It was the best fun I had ever had. And yes, of course, I missed my flight back to Brisbane.

There was an instant attraction between me and Lachlan, a handsome, reserved man I assumed was a few years older than me. There was something sweet and welcoming about him. We became very close, and I kept postponing my flight two days at a time, eventually staying with him for a week. As we lay in bed on one of those first mornings, he told me that that first night at the club he could not take his eyes off me, and not just because I was wearing no shirt and a tie (my trademark Brisbane clubbing uniform) and had dyed my sandy hair emo-black. 'My eyes were drawn to you, as if you were dancing in your own personal spotlight, like in the movies,' he told me later. 'What made you stand out for me was that you looked so happy and relaxed, just floating around, while everyone else was so intense and wearing their attitude.' He was fascinated, he said, by my warm and friendly aura, the way I was polite and smiled a lot and people gravitated to me. He couldn't believe it when someone accidentally spilled a drink on me and I laughed it off. Apparently in hyper-aggressive Sydney a spilled drink is a declaration of war. To test if I was really as easygoing as I seemed, he'd had his theatrical friend from the bus stop bang into me on the dance floor, and *I* apologised.

Lachlan and I went for walks, and he introduced me to his friends. We clubbed, dined out, and we talked endlessly … I had never met anyone I could talk with so easily as Lachlan. We had just met, yet it seemed to each of us that we'd known the other forever. We bared our souls. I trusted him and felt there was nothing I could not confide to him, including my self-harming – I showed him the criss-cross scars on my arms — and my depression and anxiety and despair at the relentless grind of diving. I told him about my tortured relationships with Hui and my mum. And by the time our week together ended he knew my entire life story, warts and all. I even told him the sad saga of Sniffy and Snuffy. Lachlan was special. I experienced many things with him that week that I had never experienced before, and I felt feelings for him I had never felt for any other man. I could be adventurous with Lachlan because I felt safe with him.

My first impressions of Lachlan, who is 10 years older than me, proved correct. He is kind, and he is wise and intelligent, the only boyfriend I've ever had who I reckon is smarter than me. (Sorry guys!) He wasn't working when I met him. He was living off his savings from a previous job. I had the distinct feeling that he would not let me come to harm. I didn't know it, but I was obviously looking for someone to look after me.

Behind his smile and generosity, I sensed a sadness within Lachlan. After a couple of days I learned why. His partner of four years, Christian, had died of cancer two years before. Lachlan had not had a significant relationship since. Nor had he worked since his partner's death. The scar of Christian's loss was still raw.

It was sad saying goodbye to Lachlan when I finally did leave for Brisbane, even though we knew we'd see each other again. We spoke on the phone for hours every night, and he sent me the money to fly down to see him the next weekend. The following weekend he came to Brisbane to visit me for a couple of days, and we decided that we wanted to live together. I told him I had no money and he said that was OK, he would pay for both of us until I started earning. A week later, he drove all the way from Sydney, his car laden with his belongings. This was serious, and it was wonderful. Suddenly there was a more powerful force in my life than Hui and diving.

We moved into a spare room in the home of my friend Alexis Paszek, who is a few years older than me and not involved in diving at all. I had met Lexi one night out on the town just a couple of months before I met Lachlan, and ever since that first night we've been really close. Hers is probably my longest-standing, most healthy friendship.

Being so happy with Lachlan made me resent diving all the more. Having him in my life gave me the strength to assert myself. Just a couple of weeks after he became my live-in partner, I told Lachlan that I was seriously considering quitting diving. He said that all that mattered was us and being happy and he would support me in whatever decision I made.

Around this time when I was mulling over my future, I took a job as a van driver delivering bottles and cans for

Liquor Land to companies throughout Brisbane. I didn't have a clock-on, clock-off time, just a set number of deliveries to make in a day. One afternoon, due to heavy traffic and other circumstances, I hadn't completed my delivery run by the time I was due at the pool for training. I was so scared that I would be in trouble with Hui that right there in the Liquor Land van I had a panic attack, crying and hyperventilating.

I managed to drive home, and to try to get my breathing back to normal I shovelled down any food I could lay my hands on in our meagrely stocked fridge. I had about 12 pieces of toast with butter and brown sugar, and a litre of milk. Eating had settled me down in the past. I lay on the floor and called Diving Australia. 'It's Matt Mitcham,' I blurted. 'I'm having a panic attack and can't come to training. Can you please tell Hui I'm going to be late?' The attack lasted an hour and then passed. Two officials came to my place to check that I was all right (or perhaps to check that I wasn't faking), and they granted me permission to take the afternoon off.

In August 2006, I walked into the Diving Australia office and told the official manning the desk that I was finished, I was done. He looked surprised and asked me if I was sure. I said I had never been more sure of anything in my life. I had to write a letter confirming that I was relinquishing my AIS scholarship, which had covered the costs of my training since I was 14. That was it. I did not say goodbye to Hui or any of the other coaches or my fellow divers. I didn't even farewell Da the duck. No one at Diving Australia tried to talk me out of my decision. Even if someone had, they would not have succeeded. I quit diving without a qualm, utterly convinced that it was absolutely the right decision if I wanted to be sane and happy.

Lachlan not only supported my decision, he was overjoyed when I walked out because he feared I was about to have a breakdown. He said I was the unhappiest person he had ever met in his life.

Lachlan and I furnished our room at Lexi's place with a thin foam mattress and we slept on that for the next few months, until we moved into a tiny flat in Fortitude Valley, conveniently close to the clubs. We held many a daytime recovery party in our flat. For the next six months we partied from Friday to Tuesday, regained our strength on Wednesday and Thursday, then headed out to party some more.

I was now officially an ex-diver and I was relishing that status. I enjoyed being a normal person. I overdid my newfound freedom and lack of commitments, and I partied to the extreme. Extreme is the way I've always done things. I was never one for moderation. When I was diving I put so much into the sport and coping with the politics of it that the whole damn thing ate me up and burned me out. When I partied, I partied to forget.

After I went to live with my grandma, Mum and I didn't see much of one another for a while, but once I turned 18 we started hanging out together a lot more. She fit right in with my friends, despite being older. She is fun and she is funny. She has a way with words that cracks me up. Instead of saying 'brag' she'll say the more obscure 'skite', and use 'parched' instead of 'thirsty', and she has some great expressions, like 'I missed out by the skin of a bee's penis' or 'I'm so hungry I could eat the arse out of a low-flying duck' (even though she's been a staunch lacto-vegetarian since she was 14). One night at the Fringe Bar in Fortitude Valley I had to rescue her from the unwanted attentions of a would-be Romeo. I could see that my mother wanted no part of this guy, so I strode up to them and chirped, 'Mum, can I have $20 for a beer?' The fellow said, 'That's your *son*?!' and hightailed it out of there. I never got to keep the $20, though.

I would send her a text at 3am asking if she was still out, and she might reply 'At Fringe Bar. Let's meet?' Or she might text me at 5am asking if I had a lift home. If I didn't, she would come to the club where I was and pick me up. There were none of the usual mother–son boundaries between us.

I had no problem with Mum joining us at the Valley gay clubs where she partied and danced with us. Lachlan did. He felt uncomfortable about the situation. Frankly, he thought our interaction was weird. Mum and I could swing from hugs to open warfare in a flash, and he couldn't deal with that. She and I thought our over-the-top theatricality was hilarious. We pissed ourselves laughing because we were making jokes of our own dysfunctions.

I wanted the two most important people in my life to get on, but Lachlan had come from a loving and conventional family, and when he saw me drinking and squabbling with Mum he thought it was strange. Lachlan took real exception when Mum and I fought, because he hated to hear anyone saying bad things to me. Because my mum and I weren't ready, or able, to deal with the pain of our dysfunctional relationship, we compensated by hurling emotional daggers at each other as payback for the damage we'd done to each other over the years.

Mum has a sharp tongue. It wasn't, however, all one-way traffic. I could trade barbs with her – and I found other ways to stir her, too. Lachlan and I were at a recovery party one time and Mum turned up. It had been a big night. She was still under the influence, and I knew she would be easily persuadable. So, just to annoy her and show everyone how funny I am, I told her to get up and take the curtain off the curtain rod. Then I told her to put it back on, and she did. I made her do this repeatedly. Everyone else was horrified at seeing the dark side of nice Matthew. It was just our little game. It was us being us.

Neither of us realised at the time that what we thought of as hilarious banter and joking really upset people; we weren't aware that people saw through them and knew that we were really conducting a kind of emotional warfare. My mum has since told me that the reason she played along and laughed was that she knew all those little emotional daggers that I was throwing at her were justified. She couldn't argue, and laughing along was her way of saying, 'Yes, I acknowledge you have the right to feel that way'. She showed her penance by accepting my emotional daggers and sharing the joke with me. It was as if we treated each other like this because it brought us closer together to acknowledge the past hurts and try to make a joke out of them. It was like we were conducting our own sort of subliminal psychotherapy. We haven't treated each other like that for a couple of years now, and I suppose it's because I don't feel that there is bad blood between us any more, so there is no need for me to throw these underhanded barbs.

Another issue was Mum's determination to come to Lachlan's and my flat to see me any time she felt like it. Lachlan objected because privacy and personal space is important to him, and he felt that by dropping in unannounced my mother was invading it. He said he thought it was fair if he was told ahead of time that Mum was coming to see me. But Mum resented not being able to make spontaneous visits and interpreted Lachlan's need for advance warning to mean that he didn't want her to see me at all. This was certainly not the case.

Lachlan, whose mother was more of a nurturing, traditional mum, also had trouble coming to terms with Mum's and my intimacy. Our theory is that it's better to know everything about each other so we can be prepared should anything untoward happen. There are no skeletons lurking in our respective closets. That was her theory behind wanting to come out clubbing when I was underage. She was supervising me (although I have to say that at times it was me who was supervising her!). We partied and danced together. We had an agreement to be absolutely open and 100 percent honest with each other about everything.

One day, at another recovery party at our place after a night's heavy clubbing, I took a large amount of LSD and went into a massive and cathartic trip. I spent eight hours in the darkened bedroom, Lachlan beside me, regressing through my life and re-experiencing all the hurt. I wept and shook and moaned as it all rushed out. I sounded like a wounded animal in deep pain and shock. I regressed so far through my memories that I went past my birth and back into my mother's life. I experienced the traumas she had told me about. I felt the pain of every memory and recounted it all to Lachlan.

For all those long hours, Lachlan held me close and told me everything was going to be OK. That catharsis completely changed the way I felt about Mum. Later, when I'd stopped crying, I no longer resented her for everything that had happened to us, or blamed her for my depression. I understood and forgave. I felt so much more mature. So grounded and centred. So much happier. Unloading to Lachlan during my LSD haze was more beneficial than all the therapy and medicating and seeking oblivion through drugs and alcohol and self-harm. Depression is the suppression of feelings, and I had stirred up the sediment of my subconscious and brought all this stuff to the surface. It bubbled away and purged my locked-away emotions in one crazy, unplanned therapy session. My experience may sound far-fetched, but up until LSD was banned in the 1960s, psychotherapists and psychiatrists had given it to tens of thousands of patients to loosen their minds and dredge up repressed thoughts and feelings.

I don't advocate drugs and I haven't done LSD since that day, yet undeniably what I went through in the dark bedroom with Lachlan changed my life. My epiphany changed the dynamic between my mum and me.

Lachlan absorbed so much of my pain, and he offered me his strong shoulder even while he was still struggling with his own sadness and painful memories in the wake of Christian's death. Lachlan and I spent our first Christmas together, in 2006, in Albury with Lachlan's family. I encouraged him to go to church and light a candle for Christian. We agreed to commemorate Christian's passing on his death day every year in this way. I told Lachlan, 'You support me, and I totally support you. If you need to talk about Christian, I'm here'. Today there is stuff in our house that was Christian's. His armchair sits in the corner of our living room, and it has now been claimed by my puppy, Louis. Just the other day I saw two glass candle holders. I asked Lachlan where they came from. He said they were Christian's and he cherished them and now they were part of *our* life.

Grandad had also met Lachlan. He came over to visit our apartment in the Valley when he was in town one day. I was a bit apprehensive about it beforehand, because it was the first time I had ever introduced a partner to anybody in the family other than my mum and I wasn't sure about grandad's generational preconceptions about me being gay, or homosexuality in general. But their meeting was absolutely the best, so much better than what I could have expected. Grandad was just wonderful and supportive about Lachlan and my relationship, and really nonchalant about us being gay.

I was even more worried about introducing Lachlan to my grandma, because I had indicated to her when I was around 15 that I was bi or gay, and she hadn't seemed 100 percent supportive. It was simply a generational thing: she felt that my life would be much easier if I was straight.

Grandma has come around to the idea, because she's seen that my life has turned out okay and that I don't have those difficulties with my sexuality that she was worried about. She's since met Lachlan and thinks he's really lovely, and she is supportive of our relationship because she's seen how well he's taken care of me.

Up until just recently, Mum, Grandma and Grandad were the only people in my family who had actually met Lachlan. Even after six years, I still have a little trepidation about introducing him to the rest of my family, even though they've all expressed how eager they are to meet him. When I try to pinpoint the source of my apprehension, I can only put it down to the subliminal message that I, and no doubt countless other young LGBT kids, picked up from society: that gay is not as good as straight. It's quite terrifying to realise that, despite all the evidence to invalidate our concerns, this subliminal message we take on as children gets so deeply rooted that it impacts what we believe about ourselves and how we live our lives for years and years.

With no diving and no school — since I had quit that too — money was scarce, especially since I was no longer entitled to a student's living away from home allowance. I had quit the van-driving job after only a couple of weeks, because I was always on edge worrying about whether I would be late. I took a job going out onto the streets of Brisbane and canvassing pedestrians to support various charities. One charity I represented helped fund research into the causes and cures of children's cancer. There was no wage; I was paid a commission representing a small percentage of each donation. I was hopeless at that job. I felt lousy convincing people who only wanted to go about their daily business to stop and hear my spiel. I knew I wasn't doing street marketing to help the sick kids – I was doing it to make money. I'm an advocate for a good many causes, but my motivation behind this charity work was impure. When I approached people on the street asking for money, it wasn't as a good Samaritan. I had 'I'm a fraud' written all over my face. I felt grubby at the end of each day, and not just because of the gritty streets. Passers-by avoided me because they picked up my negative vibe. My emo hair probably didn't help either. I only lasted a couple of weeks.

Apart from a chronic lack of money, I had a ball, making up for lost time spent hurling myself off the end of a diving board. I clubbed, did drugs and got drunk far too often, and I loved it all.

I never saw it coming. After six months of wasting myself in Brisbane, I woke up one morning missing diving. Not missing Hui and the coaches and the misery, but missing the discipline, challenge and, of all things, joy of *diving*. It was a case of the old adage: You don't know what you've got till it's gone. It was as if I had to be without diving to appreciate it. Returning to the pool at the Chandler complex was out of the question. I had well and truly burned that bridge. If only there was a way to dive seriously, expressing my talent and creativity, winning events, and yet have fun. I was a world class party boy, but, after all, diving was what I did best.

6

lifeline

Then, out of the blue, in January 2007, my phone buzzed with a text message. It was from Chava Sobrino, the head diving coach of the NSW Institute of Sport (NSWIS), who was based at the Sydney Aquatic Centre. 'Matthew, if you ever want to start diving again I'll have a place for you in my squad. Chava.' I'd always liked Chava. I had known him ever since I started diving, because he coached junior as well as senior athletes, so I met him at junior competitions.

Born in 1959, Chava had dived for his native Mexico at the 1980 Olympics in Moscow, placing ninth in his event. Then a shoulder injury took him out of competitive diving, and he became the head coach for Mexico, training some of the best divers that country has ever seen. In 1995 he moved to Brisbane with his wife, Alena, after he got an invitation from the AIS to coach divers for the Atlanta Olympics in 1996. Then in 1997, he'd moved to Sydney to become head coach for NSWIS, and he's stayed there ever since. At the Sydney Olympics his divers Loudy Tourky (now Loudy Wiggins) and Rebecca Gilmore got a bronze medal in the 10 metre platform synchro, which was actually the first Olympic medal that Australia had won in diving for 76 years.

I knew him to be a funny, compassionate guy who was always smiling and laughing. I had never seen him raise his voice or get angry with a diver; in fact, I'd never really seen him be anything other than a placid, understanding, warm, kind, caring man. He is the most social person and gets along with absolutely anybody; he's got a million and one friends and no enemies. On tour I tried to hang out with him because he preferred to find a café and eat and talk rather than shop like most of the others, and that suited me, because I was always hungry and up for a chat; besides, I never had any money for shopping anyway.

During our talks I confided to Chava my dissatisfaction with training and diving and life in general. I was sounding him out, because he always gave good advice. He listened, and by his sympathetic response, he clearly understood. When he thought it would help me deal with a particular situation, he would give me examples of how he or one of his athletes had handled something similar. Or if he could tell that my line of thinking wasn't going to go anywhere positive, he would just take my mind off the subject completely. He's got the most enormous repertoire of jokes, an absolute wealth of corny, bad jokes and puns. That's my favourite type of humour, and most of the jokes are fresh material because they're Mexican.

It occurred to me, when I'd read his text, that if I'd had nurturing coaches like Chava I may still be diving. His message was typical of the man: reaching out, no pressure, no strings, just a reminder that he respected me and was around if ever I needed him.

Someone else who called me was Sylvia Blackshaw, the mother of Kathryn Blackshaw, who dived with Chava's squad. I had spent time with the generous and hospitable Blackshaw family at their home in Croydon Park when I was competing in Sydney. Sylvia said, 'Matthew, it's such a terrible shame that you've quit. Definitely consider coming to Sydney to dive with Chava because you're too good to waste all your talent. Brisbane is not the only place to dive'.

This was exactly what I needed to hear. Chava and Sylvia were right. If I did go back to diving, I *didn't* have to dive with the coaches in Brisbane. There *were* other options open to me. Like diving with Chava in Sydney.

The excitement I felt at the prospect of diving again made me realise, without a doubt, that I had unfinished business with the sport. I had given seven years of my life to diving but had never represented my country at the pinnacle of sport: the Olympic Games. Representing Australia at an Olympics had been my dream when I took up diving. I understood now that giving diving away, as much as I felt I needed to at that time, meant nothing less than that I had wasted my teenage years. By the end of 2006, I'd given up on my Olympic dream, swapped it for a life of delicious excess, but now Chava and Sylvia had made me think. I talked to Lachlan and did some soul-searching. I called Chava back and asked him if he was serious about me joining him. He assured me he was. He said if I was prepared to convince him that I was serious about becoming an elite athlete again, and was prepared to make all the sacrifices that that entailed, he would approach Diving Australia – the national governing body that oversees all the diving programs and clubs – to have me reinstated so I could train with him at the Sydney Aquatic Centre. I told Chava that I would move to Sydney with Lachlan and find somewhere to live so that if or when Diving Australia granted its approval, I could start diving with him immediately.

I said 'See you soon' to my mum and grandma, who were both really supportive of my decision to start diving again and to train with Chava. Lachlan and I put our furniture and the belongings that we couldn't wear or fit in a suitcase into boxes and put them in storage, planning to get them out and truck them down to Sydney when we found somewhere to live. We would borrow from my grandfather and Lachlan's father to pay the removalist.

When Lachlan and I drove out of Brisbane and down the Pacific Highway in Lachlan's car, the sheriff, so to speak, was on our trail. Our partying had left us a couple of thousand dollars in debt, and we still owed about six weeks' unpaid rent on our flat. When I have money troubles, I tend to bury my head in the sand. The stress becomes too much, and I block it out. The only reason we weren't evicted was that the landlord had made it blindingly obvious that he had a crush on me and so he kept giving us extra time to pay. I'm not proud to say that I took advantage of his feelings for me and strung out our tenancy and did not pay him. When the time was right, we made our getaway, leaving the landlord angry and out of pocket.

Lachlan and I arrived in Sydney in January 2007, and, while we scoured the city for cheap accommodation and tried to save some money to pay for it, we shacked up on our photographer friend John's couch in his beautiful apartment in harbourside Watsons Bay. I am so grateful to him for his kindness. John is a grounded and mature 50-something who can still go out with younger people and have as much fun, without remotely looking out of place. When I'm 50 I hope I'm travelling as well. While Chava was holding lengthy negotiations with Diving Australia, trying to get me reinstated, we had an idyllic summer at Watsons Bay. Every day was gorgeous, free and without pressure, filled with parties at friends' places and dancing from late till dawn in the clubs of Darlinghurst. It was bliss. We swam in the tidal pool at Watsons Bay and at Camp Cove, Red Leaf and Nielsen Park beaches. We leaped off jetties into the cool green harbour. We dined outdoors in the midday sunshine or the glowing purple dusk. The cockatoos came to our balcony each day for a feast of sunflower seeds. Our friend Jonathan, an art curator who lives in Rome and returns to Sydney for the summer, joined us at John's. We whiled away drowsy morning-after hours, the four of us, drinking coffee and doing the morning crossword puzzle in the newspaper. Friends came and went. Jonathan cooked beautifully. I had never eaten so well and healthily. There was always something wonderful about to happen, and excitement in the sultry air. Amid all this beauty, drugs seemed out of place, unnecessary, and while I was still dabbling I had no need to write myself off.

I had, and still have, some wonderful older gay friends in their 40s and 50s, and I learn much from them. I came to know them through Lachlan, who is a decade older than me. Lachlan's late boyfriend, Christian, was 10 years older than him, and many of our friends now are people Lachlan had met through Christian. When I came to Sydney, I changed from a boy into a man. These guys were caring and intelligent and laughed with me, not at me, at my eccentricities and show-off ways. They supported me unequivocally, they didn't judge, having all become comfortable with their own sexuality and gone through the hoops of making their mark in a straight society. Nothing shocked them.

My relationship with Lachlan had grown even stronger and closer. When Lachlan found me he was still grieving, and he held on to me tightly because of his pain. I suppose I was a bandaid to his wounds. I embraced him, too, because he was the only person I trusted. I needed him, as he needed me, and we looked after each after.

I'd decided that when I moved to Sydney I would start my life again. Find new directions. No more concealing my sexuality. In that and every other aspect of my life I would be honest. I would be myself, and people would like or reject me for what I was, not what I achieved or did not. I have never lacked good friends since.

I had been a seething mass of insecurities. I had erected barriers, and people didn't know how to navigate the terrain of me, so they steered clear. Now that I was myself, I attracted good people. My life was so much better now. In this light, cutting myself seemed an alien, dangerous thing to do. My depression was not so all-consuming, and some days it lifted completely.

I went to see Chava soon after I arrived in Sydney. He was understanding and inspiring, and I realised that I really was ready to dive again. I was ready to achieve the Olympic dream that I had believed I'd dashed when I quit but knew now I had merely put on the backburner. My batteries were full, my mind was fresh, and if I was reinstated by Diving Australia, I would have the physical and mental strength to focus on diving, to knuckle down and train with the intensity, vigour and passion that had been ground out of me in Brisbane. Chava welcomed me with open arms, then told me what I already knew: that attaining my past form after a layoff would not be easy. However, if I succeeded, he said, 'I will hand you back your career'.

I assured Chava that I would do anything and everything he asked of me. 'You're in charge, and I trust you.'

He did things very differently to the coaches in Brisbane. 'My function,' he said, 'is to perfect your diving technique to give you the chance to win an Olympic medal. I want you to enjoy diving. I'm not going to push you. It's up to you to push yourself. If you don't want to give 100 percent, that's your problem. I'm not here to motivate you. I expect you to be dedicated. If you can't fit in here, then see you later.'

I set myself the goal of qualifying for the 2008 Olympic Games, being held in 15 months' time in Beijing, doing my best there and then making a serious bid for gold at the London Games in 2012. Of course, before any of that could happen, I needed the approval of Diving Australia.

Chava sent a barrage of calls and letters on my behalf, but he had his work cut out persuading the organisation to take me back into the fold. I understood why no one there was exactly turning handstands of joy at the prospect of my return. I didn't know what was going on behind the scenes and whether head coach Hui opposed my readmission — but if he did, I would be the last person to blame him. I had given him a terrible time while I was under his coaching. I was such a little shit. Young, silly and precious, I convinced myself that I was always the victim and Hui the aggressor. Everything that happened to me was someone else's fault. Today I understand why he dealt with me the way he did. He was only reacting in his own way. He believed he had to control me before he could transform me into a world-class diver.

Chava realised that if I was going to have even a remote chance of being selected in the Australian diving team for the Games the following year, I had to start training immediately. I began doing some covert and unofficial training with Chava and Rebecca Gilmore, who had won a bronze medal in the 2000 Olympics 10 metre platform synchro with Loudy Tourky, but there was no guarantee that I would even be allowed to compete at the Olympics. I could be diving brilliantly, but without the green light from Diving Australia, I was nowhere. A month after I came to Sydney, Chava had still heard nothing, so he called an official and begged that Diving Australia review my application, as time was running out.

'He's the best diver in Australia,' Chava said. 'He went off the rails but now really wants to get back on. I know I can help him.'

'Matthew Mitcham is trouble,' the official replied. 'If he ever makes it back on track we'll call it a miracle.'

When Chava told me what the official had said, I was more determined than ever to push myself and make every sacrifice to become again one of the best divers in the world, with or without the blessing of Diving Australia, and whether or not I was cleared to represent Australia at the Olympics or other Diving Australia and FINA events.

At one point, Chava met with Charles Turner, CEO of the NSW Institute of Sport (NSWIS). Chava laid out my diving records and also was upfront with Charles about my history. Charles asked Chava if I was really worth all the trouble that he was going to for me. Chava said I was, and assured him that I had turned over a new leaf and was determined to make the Olympics. Charles took Chava's words on board and said that, as far as he was concerned, NSWIS had a duty of care to athletes, and I had his full support in pressing for my reinstatement. 'Let's do it,' he said. From that moment on, Charles lobbied Diving Australia continually for me to be allowed to train in Sydney. His support for me has been unwavering, and I have the deepest gratitude towards him and NSWIS.

In February, Mum rang from Brisbane. I could tell from her quavering voice that something was wrong. 'I've got something to tell you,' she said. My mind raced through all the possibilities. She continued, 'I tried to commit suicide'.

It had happened months before, and she had ended up in hospital. For some time, she had been drinking alcoholically, suffering from untreated depression in addition to her Asperger's syndrome, and feeling that her life was stagnating. Then she had an argument with her boyfriend, and after that she tried to take her life. She and Grandma and Grandad had kept her suicide attempt from me at the time because I was overseas competing and they didn't want it to put me off. And then they had continued to shelter me from it, until the guilt of breaking our rule to always tell each other everything became too much for Mum and she had to call me.

Next she said, 'I have to know — do you need me any more, because if you don't, I'll feel OK if I kill myself. I won't feel as if I'm leaving you high and dry'.

I experienced a full gamut of emotions in all of three seconds. Shock: what happened to Mum to elicit suicidal actions? Betrayal: why did no one tell me this for so long?

Fury: how could she be so selfish, opting to take the easy way out and leave me to deal with her shit on my own? Indignation: how could she be so cowardly as to absolve herself of all responsibility for her own mortality? Resentment: and then have the audacity to burden her own son to choose between her unhappiness or his own. Shame: Oh my God, I'm such a hypocrite – I tried to kill myself twice as a teen, with hardly a consideration for how it would affect her. Acceptance: who gives me the right to sentence her to a life in misery for my own reasons?

She had been this depressed before, when I was a kid, but back then I knew she felt a sense of obligation as a parent to look after me. Suicide was not an option then, no matter how deep the pain of her depression, so she turned to alcohol instead. Now I had grown up, her guideline for whether she could do it or not was whether I still needed her.

My reply was a measure of how much I'd matured and acquired some wisdom. 'Mum, I don't need you … but I *want* you.'

And I *did* want her. I didn't want her to die. I was filled with sadness at the thought of not having her in my life any more. Our relationship had changed over the past year. I now saw her as she truly was: a brave woman struggling against the odds and doing the best she could to beat her demons, to survive and to be my mum.

★

It was purely for money, certainly not love, that I became a clown diver in a troupe at the Royal Easter Show at Homebush Bay. Gene Kimlin, my one-time synchro diving partner from Brisbane, was doing the clown gig with another guy, who had just pulled out. Hard as it may be to understand, dressing in an outlandish costume and doing crazy dives from a 14 metre diving board into a shallow pool to the jeers and cheers of a bunch of fairy floss-munching showgoers had lost its appeal for him. Gene asked me if I would be interested in taking his place. 'Will I get paid?' I asked hopefully.

'A thousand dollars a week for three shows a day every day for the two weeks of the Show,' said Gene.

'Two thousand bucks?' I said. 'When do I start?'

After passing my audition, I joined the troupe, which comprised clowns, synchronised swimmers, divers and acrobats dressed as policemen, insects and animals, robbers and firemen. I pulled on my costume, which happened to be a black and yellow bumblebee suit, and for my first show performed tumbles, somersaults and bombs into a narrow 2 metre deep tank from the 14 metre platform, a 5 metre platform and a 3 metre plank with hardly any spring. My job was to make everyone laugh with my antics and stunts. Stunt diving wasn't nearly as easy as it looked, and it required skill and precision to finish the show unscathed.

I performed a set routine each show. I did a simple somersault off the 5 metre platform and two tricky dives off the 3 metre plank, then the synchronised swimmers gave a display, and while they were on I changed into my bee costume and did what I called my dillies (or silly dives). I stood on the plank before the throng and declared, 'To all you honeys out there … I'm your super bee!' and then I launched myself, stretched out like Superman, before plunging into the tiny tank. After that I picked up a bucket and filled it with water. Another clown would douse me with water from his bucket then run in front of the crowd. I made like I was going to let them all have the contents of my bucket, and the crowd would scream in anticipation of a drenching, but my bucket had a false bottom so no one got wet and I waved at them through the hole in it. A couple of cartwheels and slips in front of the crowd and that was my lot.

I had only one close call. I was performing the Super Bee stunt, but I jumped too far out. In a futile bid to avoid smashing into the side of the tank, I pumped my legs as if I was riding bicycle. I got a few bumps and scrapes but the worst of it was that my pride as Super Bee was bruised.

The shallowness of the tank was always a danger, too,

even with easy dives. I had to tumble the instant I hit the water to avoid smacking the bottom.

That clown diving stint at the Easter Show was a fantastic experience and a bunch of fun. The two synchronised swimming girls were elite level synchronised swimmers on the national team whom I'd known at the AIS in Brisbane, Sarah Bombell and Eloise Amberger, affectionately known as Bum-smelly and Hamburger. They represented Australia at the 2008 Beijing and 2012 London Olympics. I had also known some of the other divers from my former life.

It was good to dive again with Gene Kimlin. He was a great diver but had been plagued by injury. He had suffered lots of ganglions, and we were training to be synchro partners at the 2006 Commonwealth Games when, in the official trials, he hit his head on the 10 metre platform. I didn't know it during the dive, because with the wind rushing past you, it's hard to hear anything. I did a really good dive, swam to the edge of the pool and when I looked back I just saw this big brown cloud of blood in the water. Another diver jumped in and dragged Gene to the side of the pool and the lifeguards pulled him out. There was blood running down his face and coagulating in his eyebrows and eyelashes. After a minute, he turned and asked me, 'So what actually happened?' And he asked me several more times, because he was so dazed. It was heart wrenching every time he asked, 'So what actually happened?'

I felt sick to my stomach, and very uneasy, but after Gene was taken away in an ambulance I went back up to the platform and did my dive again. I didn't want the seed of fear to be planted in my mind. It took me ages to get up the courage to do my dive again, because it was a reverse — one of the ones where you're susceptible to hitting your head because you're blind to the platform. When I got to the end of the platform, there were strands of Gene's hair left behind.

The next day, between our morning and afternoon training sessions, Hui gave me permission to go out and find Gene a cake — it was a bit of a mission because it had to be flourless, as he's a coeliac. Once I found one, I got the baker to pipe a special message onto the top of it: 'Jump it out, Genus!' (his nickname, because of what it rhymes with).

The injury ripped a flap of skin in Gene's scalp that required 16 stitches, and he still has a horseshoe-shaped scar in his hairline. That eliminated him from the 10 metre event. He then went all-out to qualify for the 1 metre springboard. He won the preliminary event wearing a cap to keep his scalp in place. The cap pushed all the fluid from his wound down to his eyebrows so they bulged way out. The next day when he turned up at the pool for the semi-final he had two big shiners. In the end, he didn't contest the semis. He was too busted up. Gene retired after that.

The diving money allowed Lachlan and me to rent a $325 a week one-bedroom loft apartment in Zetland, in Sydney's inner south-west. Lachlan and I didn't want to leave John's apartment at Watsons Bay, but after two months he was entitled to some privacy and we truly did need a place of our own.

After we had paid our security bond and four weeks' rent in advance, there was little money left over to live on. Because I had no money to buy my lunch, to keep hunger at bay I munched all day on the free Cornetto ice creams and Nudie ice blocks that were a perk of my Easter Show job. I also devoured as many of the free samples in the food pavilions as I could before the stallholders sent me on my way. At home, the cheapo two-minute noodles or tinned tuna that Lachlan and I devoured seemed like delicacies.

About the time that I was having so much fun doing clown dives, I realised I'd got my need to be wild out of my system. I had used it to compensate (*over*-compensate) for all the discipline of the diving years with the Chinese coaches and the strain of trying to be the good boy I wasn't to keep the peace with Mum. I went wild to compensate for not having a social life when I was younger because of the demands of diving. When I gave up diving six months before, I took off the straitjacket and replaced it with a shirtless tie or a clown suit. Good had come of my time out: I had met Lachlan and I had escaped from the pool in Brisbane. Now, in love, secure and satisfied, I felt ready to devote myself to diving again and going to the Olympics. But through February and March, I was still waiting for Diving Australia to make their decision.

The AIS program in Brisbane was the national program and understandably they wanted to gather the best divers at the pool in Chandler. Word came to me through Chava that if I was to get back into the program I would have to return to Brisbane. I dug my heels in and made it known to Diving Australia that Sydney was now my home, and Chava was the man I wanted to coach me. Those things were non-negotiable.

In April 2007, with just 15 months to go before the Beijing Olympics, all of Chava and Charles Turner's lobbying paid off and I was readmitted to Diving Australia's Olympic diving program as a member of Chava's squad. For the first three months I would be on a probationary scholarship, until I had proven that I could adhere to all the rules and give my all to training.

7

back on the 'straight' and narrow

I'll be honest, in addition to wanting to make the Olympic team for Beijing, another motivation for reclaiming my diving career was my desire to prove that Diving Australia's fears about me were misplaced. I wanted to say, 'Stuff you! You were wrong about me. I'll show you!'

I went into hard training with Chava at the Aquatic Centre, scene of so many Australian triumphs at the Sydney Games. Because I'd been unofficially training, I wasn't totally rusty. On my first day of official training with NSWIS, I was able to perform my full 1 metre list of dives. By the third day, I could do my full list of 3 metre dives, and my 10 metre dives by the end of the week. True, my form was horrible, but I performed all the right moves. I was pleased, and so was Chava. It was almost as though I had never been away, as my diving muscle memory took over. Chava told me it was most unusual to be in such an advanced position after six months away from the sport.

The list of dives that I was doing with Chava was the same list I was performing when I retired. I began re-perfecting them. Now I had ahead of me more than a year of hard training to get my act together before the Olympics. I gave Chava every ounce of dedication and focus that I had.

My mantra as I commenced every practice dive was, 'This dive has to be perfect because it is for Olympic gold'. Even though all I was trying to do was to qualify for the national team, I trained as if every dive was the dive of my life.

It shows how much I wanted to climb back onto the diving board that then and there I became straighty-180. I stopped partying and completely gave up drugs and alcohol. Chava had put so much faith in me, he had given me my career back, and being fit and well was all he asked of me. I was not about to let him down.

I turned my back on the club scene. Afraid that dance music of any kind – be it house, trance or electro pop, all music I loved – would spur a relapse, I stopped playing it. To this day, I can no longer listen to the music I danced to in those clubs. That's when my music taste changed for the better. Today I listen to a lot of indie music, folk, roots, alternative pop. Beautiful acoustic music played with real instruments, not synthesisers. I like my new music so much more.

Lachlan's and my once-raging social life had dwindled to a few snatched relaxed hours together on weekends. The Sydney club scene was having to get by without us. Lachlan sacrificed dancing and partying to be in synch with my needs. I was driven to qualify for the Olympics, so I found the transition to the straight and narrow easy. And so did Lachlan, who knew what was important to me, and that it was time for us both to rein in our excesses.

Chava assumed I was eating well away from the pool. He assumed wrongly. I didn't tell him I was broke. He would have been appalled to know that I was existing on baked beans on toast, tinned tuna and two-minute noodles, with, on a good day, a can of sweet corn mixed in. Hardly ideal fuel for Olympic training. To pay for my train fare to Homebush, I habitually plunged my hand down under the cushions of our lounge in case any coins had become lodged there.

Finally, things came to a head when Chava confronted me about why I would occasionally miss training. The truth was that I couldn't afford the train fare. I was honest with him and revealed my desperate financial situation.

As ever, Chava did all he could to help. He asked Charles Turner, CEO of NSWIS, if I could receive a travel allowance from home to the pool and back each day. NSWIS gave me $120 a week, which was a godsend.

Sarina Bratton, the mother of junior NSWIS diver Bianca Bratton and a diving competition judge, was another who came to my rescue. Since I'd joined Chava's squad, Sarina had sat in the stands and watched me train. She was impressed by my style and technique, and filmed me. When Chava told her I was skint, she offered me the job of administrative assistant at the company she founded, Orion Expedition Cruises. It specialises in luxury voyages to such places as Borneo, Japan, China, Vietnam, Arnhem Land and Antarctica. She gave me the flexibility to clock off early to go to training, and paid me $16 an hour. Thanks to her generosity, I could now afford my rent, bills and food. Things were looking up. I even got help setting up a strategic financial plan so I would be able to pay back my Queensland debts over time.

My life kicked up a good few gears. I rose at 4.30am, and Lachlan drove me to Redfern Station to catch the train to North Strathfield. There Alex Croak, one of the four divers in my training group, would pick me up on her way to the pool at Olympic Park. I trained with Chava from 6am to 8.30am, then dried off, changed and ran flat-out back to Olympic Park Station to catch a train to Lidcombe Station, where, after sprinting up and down platform stairs, I caught the train to Milsons Point, on the other side of the Harbour

Bridge. I scurried down the hill to Orion's office and spent the next few hours doing what anyone wanted me to do in the office, mainly the mail, filing and collating of travel itineraries. Because I was being paid by the hour, I made careful note of every minute I worked. I took short lunch breaks so I could log more time and earn more pay. Around 2pm, I ran back to Milsons Point Station, caught the train to Lidcombe again, went up and down the platform stairs, changed for Olympic Park and raced helter-skelter to the Aquatic Centre for a further 2½ to 3 hours' training with Chava. (They don't call that train station platform the Olympic sprint for nothing.) Then came the long train trek home to Redfern, where, around 8pm, Lachlan picked me up at the station and drove me to our apartment for a quick catch-up over baked beans on toast before I crashed and did it all again next day. It was a shattering regime, but exhilarating. I felt that my life had direction, and driving me every minute of those hectic days was my ambition to make the Olympic team. It was good to be clean and sober, to be thinking of better things than where the party was that night.

Looking back on that pre-Beijing time, I remember the exhaustion. I remember spending large chunks of every day on trains, often dozing as the stations whizzed by and sleeping through my stop. I remember noodles and baked beans.

I was over the moon to be training with Chava. I had gone back on antidepressants around the time I retired from diving, but I felt so good now that I went off them again. I was happy at heart, maybe for the first time in my life. I didn't have a single panic attack in the 15 months leading up to the Beijing Olympics. I was focused on the Games and nothing was going to stop me from being selected.

I saw flyers all around the NSWIS building looking for athletes to do speaking engagements, so I thought I'd give it a shot. I went to see their athlete career and education advisors, who asked me to deliver motivational speeches about what it takes to overcome adversity. I wrote a speech about what I had gone through in my life and how I made the transition from teenage misfit to aspiring Olympian. It must have taken me a week – the longest, seemingly most agonising week of my life – to write a 10 minute speech. The subject matter was me, so it should have been easy, but I found it impossible to write anything good about myself. It was no wonder then that I started my speech equating myself with the ugly duckling.

I stood and delivered that speech to kids in schools and clubs and to adults in corporate situations, daytime and evening, every fortnight or three weeks. To my amazement, audiences sat in silence, rapt in my every word, and then at the end they came to me and thanked me. Many said that my troubled experiences mirrored their own and I had inspired them to try to change for the better. While initially my only motivation for doing the speeches was that I desperately needed the money, they quickly took on a new significance and meaning for me when I saw that I could help people.

NSWIS placed me in their top tier of speakers. I was surprised that I was able to stand in front of an audience and inform and entertain. To some people, public speaking is a nightmare. So long as I know what I am talking about, I'm quite relaxed, and even enjoy the experience.

I, in turn, was inspired by Alex Croak. I admired her for the intensity of her training. She was the most dedicated trainer, and athlete, I had ever known. She was physically scared of diving from the 10 metre platform and she had her bad days, but she strove to overcome her fears and relentlessly pushed herself to be as good as she could be. She was also dealing with a full study load at university. Alex was my role model. I wanted to have her attitude. She's so steely and focused, yet lovely, polite and even-tempered. I even copied the way she performed her handstand dive, because she had been a gymnast and had good technique for the push.

For the next seven months I trained my guts out refining my technique. It was often tedious and repetitious work, but, thanks to Chava and my own determination not to let him down, my technique improved out of sight. I had some bad

133

diving habits I'd never been able to shake. Under Chava's changes to my style, I eliminated them.

For instance, my come-out. A come-out (or kick-out) is when you emerge from the main part of the dive and open into a straight position to line up to enter the water. My back used to be really arched during my come-out, and Chava began helping me correct the problem.

He also made adjustments to my tuck position. I used to straddle my legs wide, a bad habit ingrained in me by years of trampolining. Straddling my legs had cost me points in competitions. Because I'd been straddling my legs wide for so many years, I wasn't physically able to do the dive with my knees completely together, so I just brought them in enough that they were no longer out past my shoulders. The new knee position made it harder for me to spot − that is, orientate myself by looking at the same point each time I did a revolution − because my knees were now blocking my view. It also slowed down the rotation of my dive.

After about three weeks of diving Chava's way, I no longer straddled my knees as widely, which made a huge difference aesthetically, and my come-out was far neater. I never quite got the speed back, so to compensate, I had to jump higher. The added benefit of this was that the dive looked so much more impressive and judges would often come up to me after competitions and remark on how beautiful my jump was.

Another of Chava's changes to my style involved my top-drawer dive: a back two and a half somersault two and a half twist in the pike position. I had been prone to twisting too early, which made my trajectory crooked and put the rest of the dive off-kilter. To correct that tendency, Chava had me delay my twist and taught me to visualise two brick walls running parallel on either side of me, so when I did my jump to start the dive, I had to imagine I was launching myself into the gap between the walls and I would need to keep straight or collide with them. That worked too.

He had me repeating cue words to myself as I was preparing to dive. 'Tall' meant that when I did my take-off from the platform I had to be conscious of jumping higher, as if I actually was taller. 'Fast arms' meant that after I came out of the pike I had to straighten my arms quickly. (If you're too slow to lock out your elbows – that is, extend your arms out straight – your arms buckle when you hit the water. Your hands might punch you in the face; and because your triceps are tensed, they might get pulled or torn.) For the inward three and a half, for instance, my mantra would be 'Tall, one-two-three [somersaults], kick, fast arms'. I would repeat these key words to myself over and over again as I was standing on the end of the platform or springboard getting ready to take the plunge.

I had to plant firmly in my mind the number of twists I was going to do, so that without even thinking I did no fewer and no more. Performing a pike, I imagined my back was rounded so I could get tighter into the pike shape.

During training sessions, Chava had a video screen at poolside. A camera in the stands recorded each dive, and after a 20-second delay to allow me to get to the video screen, we could watch various views of my dive. We could analyse what I was doing right and wrong, and make any necessary corrections.

We didn't have a dry land centre for training in Sydney like they did at Chandler. We did have a general gym for weight sessions three mornings a week. On the pool deck we did our ab exercises, dry board work and somersaults onto big thick foam crash mats.

Diving is grace, and diving is strength. You need leg and core strength, and durability to ward off the effects of colliding with the water from a great height, and you need explosive power. Springboard divers tend to be heavier and slower and much more developed in the lower body than platform divers, and the strength and conditioning exercises they do tend to be slower and involve heavier weights. Platform divers tend to be smaller, faster and lighter, because the heavier you are, the more impact you take on your wrists when you go through the water. Platform divers also tend to have more fast-twitch muscle fibres, which means that they can get a lot of height taking off from the platform just by using their own rebounding body weight.

Compared to a springboard diver, a platform diver needs more plyometric-style exercises, which develop the ability to make strong, fast, explosive movements. Plyometric leg exercises can include jumping over hurdles or onto boxes – or any kind of jumping exercise, really. An example of an abdominal plyometric exercise is lying back on a Swiss ball and bouncing your legs up and down using only your ab muscles.

When you first start out in diving, coaches will train you on all the different boards to find out which you gravitate towards. Those who are naturally better at springboard or are too scared of heights to do platform will stick with springboard, while those who are not so coordinated on springboard or are physically more suited to platform will become platform divers. It's actually quite rare once you get to open competition to find divers who do both, like I did. Because I competed in both the 10 metre platform and 3 metre springboard, my training was broader than many divers', incorporating both the slower strength training as well as the faster exercises. I particularly needed to build up tricep and shoulder strength because I had a trademark handstand dive that required it. My water sessions alternated each day between the springboard and the platform.

Compared to my coaches of past years, Chava was a revelation. Not a day went by when I didn't appreciate the difference. Chava had a sense of humour. He always made me feel wanted and respected. I immediately felt part of his diving family. We even called ourselves 'the family'. I can't remember Hui ever praising me when I did well. When I asked him why he did not, he replied that if he said nothing I should assume I had satisfied him. Because of my self-esteem problems, I needed positive reinforcement. Without it, I felt even more worthless. When I dived well for Chava, he would come bounding up and let me know. Having Chava, a man I respect so much, tell me I was good made my heart sing. When I didn't dive well he would tell me in a caring way, and show me ways to do better. This was the motivation I needed. I would die before I let this man down. I've never told Chava that he is my father figure. He'll know now.

It was important to me that Chava and my fellow divers knew that I was gay. I was sick of the lies, and I didn't want to put myself in the same position in Sydney that I found myself in at Chandler, where I never said that I was gay but never said that I wasn't either, just endured the innuendoes of the others. I had felt like the odd one out, the ugly duckling, in Brisbane; but when I came to Sydney I was immediately made to feel welcome and was embraced by everybody, absolutely everybody. Chava made sure that I knew my sexuality wasn't an issue. Before, I had felt that it was, which is why I'd never really disclosed it to anybody. I'm pretty sure Chava had never had a gay diver before, but it's not like he needed practice to know what to do: he just made me feel like it was a non-issue and that I was right to be who I am.

Being upfront worked: my sexuality was neither here nor there, and from the first at training we cracked gay and straight jokes. At first, Chava, coming from what he called a 'sheltered' upbringing in his native Mexico, was a little discomfitted by the outrageous and often non-politically correct jokes of his divers. Today we've worn him down and he thinks they're hilarious and contribute to our happy training environment. When I'm up there on the 10 metre platform, Chava yells at me, 'Come on, Matthew, dive ... don't be a poof!' And after I've performed the dive, he'll call out to a straight diver perched up there so high above the pool, 'Come on, dive ... don't be a heterosexual!' We have affectionate little nicknames for each other. His nickname for me is Puto. We all call him Cabron.

Money was always tight, but thanks to the backing of NSWIS, I was able to travel to take part in competitions around Australia; and when it came time to compete overseas, Diving Australia would cover the travel costs. My first official competition against other divers since getting back up on the platform was the South Australian State Championships in December 2007. I was up against some of my old Brisbane teammates and a number of Sydney and Athens Olympians and Melbourne Commonwealth Games divers, such as Robert Newbery and Mat Helm. I beat Robert and Mat and went on to dive at the Australian National Championships, also held in Adelaide, in January 2008. The Nationals were the first of a number of national and international events crucial to the selection of the Olympic team.

At the Nationals, I placed first in the 10 metre platform, first in the 1 metre and first in the 3 metre springboard events, making me only the fourth diver in history to win all three disciplines at the National Championships.

At the time, an ABC–TV reporter said, 'Mitcham's success in Adelaide marks the start of a long road of competition which he hopes will peak in Beijing'.

To which I replied, 'This is just the first stage. We have to qualify again in the Olympic trials then if I come top two there I have to go to Canada, America and get a certain score and a certain placing there, so I have more stages to get through to qualify'.

Soon after, in the Olympic trials in Hobart, I placed first in the 3 metre and also in the 10 metre. In February at the Beijing Olympic complex, in the Olympic diving pool inside that glorious great big blue cube, I came fifth in the 10 metre platform. I was not disappointed. In fact, I was really pleased, because I had come fifth in that same World Cup event in Beijing two years before, with years of training under my belt, and now, after a long lay-off and only a short time with Chava, I had equalled that performance. I truly didn't expect to fare so well at this stage of my comeback.

At the FINA Grand Prix in Shenzhen, China, in March, I placed third in the 10 metre platform and the 3 metre events. Quite frankly, these results blew my mind. I had never done so well as to win a bronze medal in an individual event in my life before, only in synchro events.

I was disappointed in Canada in May at the Montreal FINA Grand Prix, when I could gain only a fifth in the 10 metre platform and a fourth in the 3 metre springboard.

Later that month at the World Cup meet in Fort Lauderdale, Florida, I competed in the 10 metre platform event outdoors in a gusting wind. I have a profound distaste for diving outdoors. Usually I spot the lights on the ceiling to help me know where I am in the middle of my dive. Outdoors, of course, there is no ceiling or downlights to take bearings from. Without the usual touchstones, you can get disorientated. When you dive indoors, the water is a different colour from the ceiling, whereas, of course, the water in an open air pool reflects and so is exactly the same colour as the sky, this day a deep blue. Worse, wind plays havoc with a handstand dive. The pool is right between the Fort Lauderdale marina and the beach, exposed to coastal winds, which are strongest in the afternoons, when the finals are held. There is a flag on the 10 metre platform to tell divers, judges and spectators the wind strength. This day the flag was being blown straight out and vibrating so hard that it snapped and cracked in the wind, which also plastered my long fringe to my face. It's hard enough to balance backwards on your hands 10 metres above the water without wind, but *with* wind it's infinitely harder. In the final, a big gust knocked me so far off balance that I came down from my handstand. I put my hand up, the official signal divers use to ask for a restart. It was up to the referee to decide whether wind was a factor, and to my relief he let me proceed without a penalty. I had an ordinary preliminary event and an average semi-final in Fort Lauderdale, but an excellent final, which I won. To win a gold medal in an individual event was freaking awesome. I dared to hope that if all went according to plan at the Beijing Games, why, I might even bring back a bronze medal.

8

beijing bound

Chava was delighted with my progress. The Fort Lauderdale performance was heartening because not only was I awarded four perfect 10s by the judges on my fourth dive, but I beat a couple of the much-favoured Chinese divers, including the brilliant Zhou Luxin, everyone's pick for 2008 Olympic gold. The Chinese divers were considered the very best in the world, with Australia in second place. Chava told me not to get too cocky about defeating the Chinese at Fort Lauderdale, though, because they are not at their best when diving outdoors either.

I was progressing well and peaking (get it?) at the right time for Peking (as Beijing was once called). In June, I completed my Olympic preparation by claiming silver medals in the 10 metre platform dive at the FINA Grand Prix events in Madrid and Rostock, Germany.

The Australian diving team for the Beijing Olympic

Games was announced in June at a press conference at Chandler, and I was in it. It was sweet justice that the official Diving Australia endorsement of my comeback should take place at the very pool where I had had so many unhappy memories. Apart from feeling enormous pride and a sense of vindication, I was calm that day. To be truthful, I was not surprised to have made the team, because I had known for a long time that if I performed well at all the lead-up events – and I had done – I would qualify. It was meant to be.

Lachlan, Mum and my grandma were all noting my progress with growing hopes that something special, something we could not have imagined a few months before, was gathering. They were so supportive. Whether I was doing well or doing crap, they always had my back.

In spite of Chava's confidence that I could win a medal at the Beijing Games, going into the Olympics I thought that I might just make the final in my favoured 10 metre platform event if things went very well for me. I was putting my self-defence mechanism into effect, downplaying my chances in Beijing, against all the evidence that I would do very well. That's just the way I am. I try my best but expect to fail. That way I'm never going to be disappointed.

Leading up to Beijing, even though I trained for both the 3 metre springboard and 10 metre platform events, Chava and I both knew that my best hope of a medal was in the latter event. We continued to perfect the six 10 metre platform dives I would do at the Games.

Sarina Bratton was delighted by my selection. I owed her so much. Without her, and without Chava, I would not have made it back. Sarina excused me from work in June, just a couple of months before the Games, so I could concentrate on diving. She was so excited at my selection in the Australian team that she sent out a press release to her clients announcing that her admin assistant was off to Beijing wearing green and gold. It read, in part, 'Matt is one of the most talented divers I have ever seen. Talent, however, only gets you so far. It is hard work combined with good attitude, mental strength and determination that will see him on that winner's dais. Matt is in full time training now and not coming back to work until after the Olympics – hopefully with a medal around his neck!'

Right then I was in the news for another reason: suddenly all of Australia knew that I was gay. My coming out announcement was in no way planned. The *Sydney Morning Herald* was publishing a series profiling Beijing Olympians, and when sportswriter Jessica Halloran called and requested an interview, I was instructed by Diving Australia to comply. I found Jessica to be really sweet, and she had done her research thoroughly. She and I were going through all the run of the mill questions – How old are you? Where do you live? Who do you live with? – and because I was determined to be always honest about myself, I told her I lived with my partner ... whose name was Lachlan.

Jessica's eyes lit up. There being so few openly gay athletes, she had just struck journalistic gold. She said, 'Tell me more about your partner'.

'We've been together for nearly two years,' I said.

She asked me if I minded her putting Lachlan in the feature. I knew that if I said no, she wouldn't do so. Jessica told me to go away and think hard about whether I wanted to effectively come out in her article, and to contact her with my decision on whether the gay revelation should be retained or deleted from the profile.

So I asked Lachlan, and he gave me his blessing to have our relationship revealed in the *Sydney Morning Herald*. I also asked friends whose opinion I respected. Some said, 'Don't risk it,' and others, 'Do it!' I went for it.

In the end, although I knew very well that some sponsors might shy away from me, I thought it was better that Australians knew who was representing them and who they were supporting. Anyway, if I won anything in Beijing, the media spotlight would be well and truly on me; inevitably, my sexuality and life with Lachlan would be revealed, and it may look as if I wasn't proud of being gay and sharing my life with a wonderful man. Better to come out publicly now in the *Herald* than appear as if I'd been dragged kicking and screaming from the closet.

I phoned Jessica and told her to go right ahead and publish the whole story, including that I am gay. She was thrilled. 'Matthew, I really think the Australian public will get behind you on this. They'll support and respect you. Gay people have come out *after* the Olympics, but few have ever done so before.'

Jessica was right. After the story was published in the *Herald* and its Melbourne counterpart the *Age*, the Australian public backed me totally. The Facebook page that had been created for me swelled with friends, from 11,000 to 20,000. I had been expecting a backlash. There was not a single shred of negativity from any quarter.

The article also touched on my struggles with depression and anxiety. I'd told Jessica that without facing those challenges, I probably wouldn't have made it to the Olympic team. She quoted me saying:

'I probably wouldn't have as much of a fighting spirit ...
The more you have experienced, the more you have to draw
off. I look at the last 20 years as a long, winding path of
lessons and some hardship. I hope the rest of my life isn't
straight because that could be boring. I hope it continues to
wind, but maybe not so tumultuous. I hope I do have a long

*and winding path and more lessons to learn. I look forward
to that.'*

The rest of the media publicly accepted my sexuality, too.
I was even included in a *Who* magazine feature celebrating
Australia's sexiest Olympians. Typically, my low self-esteem
convinced me that the editors had chosen me because they
needed a token gay. When I questioned them, they protested,
'No, you've got a great body!'

'Fair enough then!' I said, with a grin.

Australian Olympians receive two reserved guest tickets for
their events. Having sacrificed so much for me and been such
a massive support, Lachlan deserved to be there to watch
me compete in Beijing. I was determined to find a way to
get him to China. Neither of us could afford his fare or
accommodation, even if we pooled our resources, so when
I learned that the Johnson & Johnson company was offering
$5000 Family Support grants to allow family members and
partners of deserving Olympians to accompany their loved
one to Beijing, I applied. Applicants had to write a story
saying why their partner should accompany them to Beijing,
and I wrote how Lachlan had been at my side through my
depression and my split from Diving Australia and right
throughout my comeback. I wasn't sure that J & J's generosity

extended to *gay* partners, and my fears seemed justified when our names were not included in the published list of those who had been awarded a grant, all of whom, I noticed, were straight. Maybe, I figured, we'd missed out because J & J was such a straight arrow family company and didn't want to be embroiled in controversy by helping gay people. When it became known that we'd missed out, there were cries of discrimination in the gay community, and one couple – whose names were both John – offered to give us $5000 so Lachlan could be with me. Happily, however, we then discovered that J & J *had* approved us for a grant but due to an administrative glitch our names hadn't made it onto the list. Lachlan and I would celebrate our two-year anniversary during the Games.

Then came more good news. Mum, of course, wanted badly to be poolside at Beijing, but she was as broke as Lachlan and me, and none of us could come up with a way to raise the funds. Just then, the gay couple John and John – Lachlan and I called them 'the other J & J' – who'd offered to send Lachlan, said, 'Well, Lachlan is going, so why don't we fund your mother?' The $5000 was sufficient to pay for Mum to be in Beijing for the two days of my 10 metre platform event. I will always be thankful for John and John's kindness, just as I will be for Johnson & Johnson's.

★

When I was training and diving in Brisbane, before each diving competition I would be given a strategic plan by my coaches. It broke down each dive in each event, and the likely outcomes of my opponents' dives, in minute detail. Chava, yet again, had a different philosophy, and one that suited me better. He instilled in me that I could not control how my rivals performed, and therefore my placing. All I could do was the best six dives that I was capable of, and if I achieved that, then my placing in the event would take care of itself. This released an enormous amount of pressure, because when I stress about factors over which I have no control my diving suffers. Also, I have always feared that if I over-analyse a dive, or even a life situation away from the pool, I'll inadvertently sabotage myself. Chava knew that this all-you-can-do-is-your-best philosophy was the right strategy for me. It was behind my training ploy to try to make *every* dive the best I had ever done.

In competition, a panel of seven judges give a score between zero and 10 points for each dive, in increments of half a point. The score takes into account how well you perform all the stages of the dive. First the judges take your approach into account. This is everything you do between taking your starting position and then launching yourself into the air on your take-off. Take-off is judged on how well you control your movements and whether you leave the board or platform

The 'money shot'. Beijing Olympic Games 2008.

© Getty Images

At the Beijing Olympics acknowledging the crowd after 'the dive' about half a second before the scores came up and I lost the plot.

```
MITCHAM MATTHEW  AUS
10 10 9.5 10 9.0 9.5 10

DIVE SCORE: 112.10
TOTAL SCORE: 536.40
RANK: 1
```

© AFP / Getty Images

My training partner Alex Croak with an appropriately profound statement for the moment: 'Oh my God, you just won the bloody Olympics.'

© AFP / Getty Images

My coach Chava's face = Gold.

Looking up at my mum, Lachlan and a few officials from Diving Australia during the medal ceremony. It was so nice to have them there for this special moment … Look how cool those bubble walls were!

This is my medal!! The photo on the left shows the side of the medal that remains consistent throughout all the Olympic Games, displaying the Greek goddess of victory Nike inside a stadium. On the other side Beijing went all out and embedded a ring of jade into every medal. The gold medals had a ring of white jade, the rarest and most valuable. Silver medals had a pale green mottled jade ring, and bronze medals had dark green jade. The lanyard was made from a delicate silk that began to fray if the wearer jumped around too vigorously. Like I did.

© Reuters / Wolfgang Rattay / Picture Media

Patriotic post-ceremony victory lap. (This is where I gave Lachlan a hug and the NBC commentator said, 'Did he just kiss that guy?!')

Closing Ceremony funsies in Beijing, 2008.

Nat Cook (beach volleyball)

Me

Robert Newbery (diving)

Bree Cole (diving)

Chantelle Newbery (diving)

Melissa Wu (diving)

Scott Robertson (diving)

Libby Trickett (swimming)

Ben Wilden (trampolining)

Sam Simpson (gymnastics)

Kate Allen (rowing)

My friends and I set up a Facebook group called 'Hahn Super Dry Challenge' to try to yield as many of these bottle tops as we could find. Obviously I didn't participate in the drinking – I just offered a pair of speedos or a lap dance to each lucky winner.

Q. WHO ACHIEVED THE HIGHEST SINGLE-DIVE SCORE IN OLYMPIC HISTORY IN BEIJING?

A. MATTHEW MITCHAM

Colonial First State Sports Performer of the Year Awards 2008. Beating the other ridiculously over-achieving athletes up for the award was a coup in itself.

You know you've made it when you've been cartoonised. Brett Willis' creations to commemorate my victory in Beijing.

Having Harbour Party 2009 stopped for everyone to sing 'Happy Birthday' to you = **BEST 21st EVER.**

Dressing up as a unicorn for the Lady Gaga concert … because a unicorn without a horn would be pointless.

Becoming an ambassador for the Federation of Gay Games. Pictured with other gay sporting legends: Michelle Ferris (cycling, AUS), Leigh-Ann Naidoo (beach volleyball, RSA) and John Amaechi (basketball).

Being supported by friends at the 2010 Mardi Gras Parade in Sydney. Rather than sitting in the back of a convertible like every other Chief of Parade, Lachlan built a platform onto a ute tray so I could jump around like a lunatic while the songs 'Black and Gold' by Sam Sparro and 'Band of Gold' by Freda Payne blared out the speakers.

With Ruby Rose and Louie Spence (my co-hosts for Arena's coverage of the 2010 Mardi Gras parade).

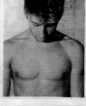

'Cross' by Maree Azzopardi, part of the Matt Dive Gold exhibition.

© Maree Azzopardi

© Renato Grome

'Metamorphic Matt' by Renato Grome, also included in the Matt Dive Gold exhibition.

Thank You Mum & Dad, for making me just the ~~way~~ GAY I am.

For the thisisoz.com.au campaign, 2009. The brief was to be photographed with a message for pro-diversity so to quote the wise and wonderful Lady Gaga, 'I was born this way!'.

MATT MITCHAM
Olympic gold
medal-winning diver
"I wish for every person
to have the option to
marry if they wish – no
matter their sexual
orientation. We have
emotionally developed
as a nation and we
are ready for this." ▶

SUPPORT
MARRIAGE
EQUALITY

I DO

BONDS

Photo by Julie Adams for *marie claire* magazine Australia

For the *marie claire* 'I Do' campaign, 2012. The push for
marriage equality in Australia gained some momentum
this year. Yes – all you progressive, open-minded people
of the future – we were still trapped in the 1900s in 2012.

With my trampoline coach Melanie Tonks sitting on a Double Mini Tramp (the apparatus I won gold for at the World Age Games, 2004).

Visiting my cousins during the Brisbane floods, making the most of having no power by playing our own smart phones. Such a floody great night!

I met my dad for the first time just before the Commonwealth Games in 2010. After meeting the rest of his family at Christmas later that year, my stepmum Yolande decided to add me to the family on the back of the 4WD. There aren't any divers in the 'My Family' sticker range, so she painted me using correction fluid based on Brett Willis' cartoon. How cute is that?!

Visiting one of my other families, the Williams. They're such a musical family that they all play one instrument or another. Now I was finally able to join in the family jam! 'Ok, uke solo time.'

Bags packed and ready to leave. I have a feeling my puppy Louis is trying to tell me something, I just don't know what it is.

Australia's formal attire for the 2010 Commonwealth Games in Delhi, India. Have you ever seen so much 'smizing'* in one picture? *smize : smile with the eyes.

The swag of silver medals I brought back from Delhi 2010. I'm pretty proud of them – they're probably my *second* greatest achievement to date.

Training at the New South Wales Institute of Sport, using the hypoxic unit which deoxygenates the air to simulate training at high altitude, making you fitter quicker.

After tearing a massive hole in my rectus abdominus (6-pack) in 2011, my physiotherapists tried to take some of the stress off the muscle with this fluoro-coloured tape. I was in a particularly ONJ (Olivia Newton-John) mood… 'let's get physical, physical!'

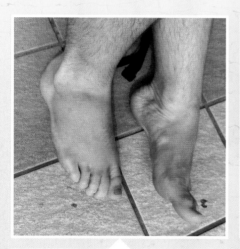

I had a couple of hideous training accidents in the lead up to the London Olympics in 2012. This was the result of hitting both feet on the platform so hard that they ballooned out and turned every ugly colour that isn't in the rainbow. To add insult to injury, I face-planted into the water and gave myself a nose bleed.

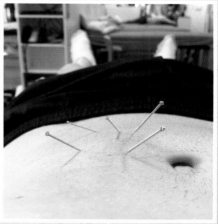

I spent so much time at the physiotherapist throughout 2011 and 2012. Here, they inserted acupuncture needles into my ab in an effort to break up the scar tissue and stimulate the growth of new muscle tissue.

Photo by Terry Trewin, courtesy of Funky Trunks

Stunning shot from a Funky Trunks campaign. These guys have been wonderful support, sponsoring me since 2009.

at the right angle for the particular dive. Elevation is the next part that's scored. The higher your elevation, the more time you have in the air to execute a good dive. Execution is the actual dive, and judges evaluate your technique, accuracy, form and how graceful you are. Entry is the final element, and the aim is to enter the water vertically and cause as little splash as possible.

The two highest and two lowest scores of the seven judges are discarded, and the three middle scores are added up. Then that number is multiplied by the degree of difficulty (DD) of the dive, to arrive at your final score. The DD is set by FINA, the world governing body for diving and other water sports. It ranges from 1.2 to 4.1, and goes up in one-tenths.

The challenge is to have a list of competition dives with a high degree of difficulty, which result in a higher score, but not to make the dives so difficult that you risk stuffing up. Usually you score more points for performing a simple dive perfectly than failing to achieve a super-difficult dive.

Because most of the dives I would perform in Beijing were only of moderate difficulty, I was relying upon a high standard of execution. My first dive would be a front three and a half pike, with a degree of difficulty of 3.0. My second would be a back three and a half tuck, with a DD of 3.3. My third dive would be an inward three and a half tuck, with a DD of 3.2. My fourth, a reverse three and a half tuck, had a

DD of 3.4. My fifth dive would be an arm-stand back double somersault with a one and a half twist in the free position, with a DD of 3.2. And my final dive – my best dive, my most difficult dive – would be the back two and a half somersault two and a half twist pike. As for degree of difficulty, at the 2008 Olympic Games, FINA rated the incredibly challenging dive at a high 3.8 points. For the 3 metre springboard I was yet to settle on a list of dives and would be testing out a range of options up until the Games.

I've always taken inspiration from any source that works for me, so in the last months before Beijing I devoured Greg Louganis's autobiography *Breaking the Surface*, hoping for a few insider's tips and insights that may help me in Beijing. It was a good read. He and I had similarities: we were divers; we were gay; we had overcome demons, including drugs. Greg would dive to the rhythm of a song in his mind. Performing a similar function for me were my cue words – those rhythmic, sequential words that I had imprinted on my brain through repetition in training and which morphed into muscle memory when I dived: 'down, down … up … punch … tall … two and a half twist … round pike …' What we didn't have in common was that Greg Louganis had twice nearly killed himself hitting his head on the diving board and the platform; hopefully a bad accident is something we will never share. Another thing that separated us – and, I thought, probably always would – was that Greg had won an Olympic gold medal.

I was still great friends with Lexi, who Lachlan and I had lived with for a time in Brisbane. She has always been super-supportive of me. Just before I flew to Beijing with the Australian team, she made me sign the back of her mobile phone case so she could be the first to have the autograph of the gold medal winner! We both had a good old laugh at that.

9

gold

August, 2008. I was in China, about to dive for Australia at the Olympic Games. I had been competing in international events for years now. Nothing prepared me for this. There was a tangible excitement in the hot, humid air. Making it all the more dramatic was the smog. You couldn't see for more than 100 metres. I had the impression that I had landed on another planet.

I wish I could say I took time to reflect on my achievement in qualifying for the Olympics – unfortunately I was too dazzled by the sights and sounds and the amazing football-pitch-sized food hall of the Olympic village. All I could do was look around and go 'OM effing G'. If I fared well in my events then there would be plenty of time for reflection.

I was the only openly gay male competitor. There were, I understand, ten out and proud lesbians at those Games ...

and one male. Me. Like Daffyd in *Little Britain*, it seemed I was the only gay in the village. Statistically, of course, this is nonsense. There were around 11,000 athletes at Beijing, and if you use the well-accepted but extremely conservative yardstick that one in 10 people is gay, there were as many as 1089 athletes secretly flying the rainbow flag. I can understand perfectly why a gay man might not want to expose himself to a macho male athletic culture, inviting persecution and costing himself sponsors, but, really, it's all so sad.

The Games village was state of the art, really cool, and had a community feel. There were rows and rows of specially built identical eight-storey apartment complexes set around parks. The place was buzzing with thousands of athletes from all over the world, a riot of noise and colour.

The Australian divers' apartment was on the eighth floor. I shared a bedroom with Robert Newbery, and Scott Robertson and Mat Helm were in another, our bedrooms separated by a living room. In mine I arrayed along my windowsill the books I had brought to while away the down time. To provide inspiration, there was Greg Louganis's *Breaking the Surface* and *Mao's Last Dancer* by Li Cunxin, both about men who beat enormous odds to succeed; and for escapism I had a book whose name I forget now, which comprised a bunch of Tim Burton-style spooky fantasy short stories about corpses, curses and zombies falling in love. I also took along *Holding the Man* by Timothy Conigrave, a book that tells the story of a man who loses his partner to AIDS. It was beautiful and so sad, and I couldn't finish it. I didn't want to cry.

The female divers bunked two to a room as well, as did the head coach, Hui Tong, and the team manager. Because there were only a certain number of beds in the Olympic Village, Chava and Xiangning Chen (Brittany Broben and James Connor's coach) had to stay offsite until the final days of the Games, when members of the Olympic tennis team had left. There were two bathrooms and a tiny fridge to keep our energy drinks cold in the living room, but no kitchenette, so there was no food preparation in the apartment. We ate in the vast food hall in a massive 100 metre wide marquee, which was a blast, and offered every kind of food: Chinese, of course, and Italian, Indian, Asian, halal, African, western, even McDonald's.

In some other places where I had competed, there was a strong military presence to deter terrorists, but Beijing was relaxed — at least it seemed so to me — and we could pretty much come and go as we pleased. I suspect that there was a massive and heavily armed security force ready to pounce at the first hint of a terrorist strike, but it was hidden from the world.

The Beijing National Aquatics Centre, or Water Cube — actually, it's rectangular — which was built especially for the Olympics, is a stunning construction. The steel structure is clad in 4000 air-filled blue 'bubbles' made of a high-tech building material (ethylene tetrafluoroethylene) that let in the sunlight. If you poked a bubble it felt spongy, and when you flicked one it went *ping*. At night, lights from within the Water Cube turned the entire building a vibrant, iridescent dark blue; and in the opening and closing ceremonies, the cube put on a swirling, spectacular rainbow-hued light show. It was far and away the most astonishing and fabulous aquatic complex I have ever dived in, a place that functionally was as good as it looked, a place that made you want to succeed.

The Chinese divers were favoured to win gold, and maybe silver as well, in all eight of the diving events to be contested. There is a maximum of two divers from any one country in each event, and if China had been allowed more, they would have been tipped to win bronze as well. I was competing in the 3 metre springboard and the 10 metre platform events, and because of my excellent showing in the recent Fort Lauderdale 10 metre event, I was ranked among the medal contenders. I had serious doubts. The red-hot field in the 10 metre platform event included world-class Chinese divers Zhou Luxin and Huo Liang, British boy wonder Thomas Daley, Gleb Galperin of Russia and my team-mate Mat Helm, who had won a silver medal at the 2004 Olympics in Athens. I felt there was the remote possibility of my winning a bronze medal if all my stars aligned and those of my fellow competitors did not. Chava remained convinced I could do better.

Chava and I rarely have arguments. Chava doesn't get angry with anyone. Rather than shout at a diver, he will just exude disappointment. All his mannerisms change and he'll shake his head and make you feel guilty. It's a much more effective motivator than losing his temper, because no one wants to make Chava disappointed. But weeks before we left for Beijing, Chava and I actually had an argument over my medal prospects. I told him what I was telling myself: that I wanted to make the final, at least not embarrass myself, and then go all out for gold in the 10 metre and 3 metre events at the London Olympics in four years' time. I was going to the Beijing Games mainly for the experience, I said. My big Olympics would be in London in 2012. Chava knew this was my self-protection mechanism taking effect: if you don't aim too high there is less chance of failure. His eyes flashed and, so rare for this calm and genial man, he was suddenly furious with me. He said if I went into competition in Beijing with that attitude I would fail. 'You're going to win a medal,' he said. 'It doesn't matter what colour. Go all out! You never know what can happen in the future. This is your time.'

In each of my events, there would be three rounds, and we would perform six dives each time. The full complement of 30 divers would do battle in the preliminary round, then the best 18 would progress to the semi-final. The 12 who performed best in the semi would compete in the final.

My first event was the 3 metre springboard, and because I was a nervous wreck, I stuffed it up. In the preliminary, I scored 439.85, way below my best, which gave me 15th place out of 29. I progressed by the skin of a bee's penis, as Mum would say, to the next stage. In the semi I did worse than I had in the preliminary, scoring 427.45 and coming 16th. So that was it for me; I was eliminated. Sometimes in the past, my nerves have sharpened my form but not this time. That night, I was inconsolable. I hid in my bedroom and cried. Someone told Chava I was in a bad way and he – wisely, as it turned out – decided to let me work through my disappointment on my own, eliminate it from my system so I could give the 10 metre platform event my best shot. I dried my eyes and went to bed after texting with Mum and Lachlan.

Next day, Chava confessed a big secret: he had sacrificed the 3 metre event for the 10 metre platform. Because I had started training later than desirable in the lead-up to the Games, there simply hadn't been time to perfect both. He knew I was underprepared for the 3 metre springboard, but hadn't said anything. 'The 3 metre is over. You should now concentrate every bit of your energy and commitment on the 10 metre event,' he said. 'The 10 metre platform is in three days. Your arse is mine. From now until then you'll do what I say. When I say eat, you eat. When I say sleep, you sleep. If I say get a massage, get a massage. It will be a time of dedication and discipline.'

I put myself in Chava's hands. Knowing it was my attack of nerves that had made me crash and burn in the 3 metre, when the 10 metre event was in full swing he focused on relaxing me. He told me to *enjoy* the event. He was loose and laidback, and consequently so was I. Again and again, he reminded me of our strategy: If I simply did my best and didn't worry about my rivals or the judges, then the results would take care of themselves.

In the 10 metre preliminary event, on August 22, I came second, but my 509.60 score was a long way behind Zhou Luxin's winning 539.80. Whatever, I was through to the semi-final the following morning. I slept well, satisfied with my performance. I was not in the slightest bit fazed by having learned that seven of the eight diving events had now been decided, and, as expected, the Chinese had won the gold in every one. The host nation was already celebrating a 10 metre platform gold medal for Zhou Luxin or Huo Liang, and consequently an Olympic diving clean sweep.

In the semi-final and final rounds, the scores start back at 0.00, and the divers compete in reverse order, so the lowest qualifier dives first and highest qualifier dives last. Next morning in the semi, I came second again, this time to Huo, who scored 549.95 to my 532.20.

So I was in the final, to be held that same evening. I was up against Huo and Zhou, Thomas Daley, Mat Helm, Gleb Galperin, Cuba's Jose Guerra, David Boudia and Thomas Finchum of the USA, Juan Uran of Colombia, Germany's Patrick Hausding and Rommel Pacheco of Mexico.

I returned to the Olympic village to eat and sleep. I was too pumped to doze off, so I lay on my bed just thinking about how momentous this all was. I was in an Olympic final. Did I really have a chance of a medal? I thought it through. In the preliminary, I had been bested only by Zhou, and then only by Huo in the semi. So, if form was any guide, I typically reasoned, they would take the gold and silver, and, with a little luck and some bloody good diving, the bronze would be mine. Being a glass half empty kind of guy, I chose not to ride the more positive train of thought that, while I had been beaten by both Chinese divers in the earlier events, *I had also beaten each of them*. It didn't occur to me that if I beat them both again, at the same time, I would be on my way to winning the event. I imagined myself up on the platform and the bronze medal being draped around my neck, and the thought overwhelmed me. The words kept pounding in my head, 'Oh my God … I can win a bronze medal!' Chava, Mr Glass Half Full, unbeknown to me, was texting his friends with a similar message, though with one big difference, 'Oh my God! He can win gold. He can do it, he can do it!'

In the afternoon, Chava took Alex Croak and me to the pool where the 10 metre event was to be held. His plan was to chill me out. We did not treat that pool reverently. We did crazy dives off the platform into the water, and we horsed around, taking underwater snapshots, splashing and laughing. The sports psychologist from the USA team came up to Chava and asked if we'd finished competing. When he told him I had a final in a couple of hours, the poor guy looked confused. But Chava knew exactly what he was doing. Having fun made the time fly. My list of six dives for the final had been set a while ago, and Chava and I were confident I would perform them well, so long as my nerves didn't unravel me as they had in the 3 metre springboard. This was better preparation at this stage than psyching myself up, planning strategy, visualising a win. With the final just hours away, I was feeling on top of the world and couldn't wait to compete.

What with messing about in the pool, chatting and laughing and listening to Amy Winehouse on my iPod, that afternoon flashed by and suddenly it was time. *My Olympic final.* I would be the 11th of the 12 finalists to dive in each of the six rounds. After six dives had been completed, the judges would tally the scores, and the diver with the highest would win the gold medal, the second highest take the silver and the third place-getter the bronze.

Minutes before the final, Chava told me, 'You're in a good moment, just enjoy everything. I don't care about the result. I want only for you to do your very best, and the results will take of themselves'.

The only thing I'm superstitious about is having any superstitions. If any start to creep up on me, I do my best to quash them. Chava, though, went to watch the finals from his 'lucky position' by the poolside. Every time he had been in that spot, I had dived well. Just then, an official Chinese photographer came and stood in front of him, blocking most of his view. He wouldn't move, and nor would Chava, because he didn't want to jinx me. I found out later that he only saw glimpses of my dives.

My first dive in that final was OK, not great, and won me just 73.50 points. At the end of the first round, I was placed ninth out of 12. I didn't panic. For my second dive, a backward three and a half somersault, four of the judges gave me 10s, and this elevated me to second place. My third dive wasn't anywhere near what I was capable of, and I slipped back to fourth, 26 points behind local hero Zhou Luxin, who was in first place. Still, I was hanging in there, feeling happy, relaxed and focused as I completed my fourth and fifth dives. They were all fine, and clawed me back into medal contention. The bronze was looking a possibility.

We gathered at the foot of the platform for our final dive. By now I was second behind Zhou, who was a massive 32.50 points ahead of me. Nobody would have bet against Zhou winning gold. He was a diver who was unaffected by pressure and could be counted on to score his usual 90 or so points. If he did, even a perfect dive from me or any of the other competitors would not be sufficient to beat him.

As Zhou mounted the platform, the locals were already celebrating another Chinese victory. When he performed his final dive I averted my eyes. I couldn't bear to watch. I heard him hit the water, and waited for the inevitable cheers of the Chinese fans to resound through the Water Cube. There were no cheers. Instead, Zhou's followers let out a loud collective crestfallen sigh. '*Ohhhhhh* …' I knew immediately that Zhou had not dived well – but I couldn't afford to allow his failure to make me complacent and influence how I dived, so I stuck my fingers in my ears and went '*la-la-la-la-la*' to block out the crowd sound.

The judges awarded him just 74.80. Not an amazing score, but he was still a whopping 107.30 points ahead of me, and Huo Liang and Gleb Galperin remained in the running, just behind me. A tremendous dive from either could win them medals, and I would be left among the also-rans. (I didn't know any of this at the time. While I had taken the occasional glance at the leader board in between rounds to check my progressive ranking, I certainly wasn't counting scores and working out complex mathematical equations in my head as I was preparing for my next dive.)

To get ahead of Zhou I needed a majority of the judges to award me perfect 10s. I was glad I had left my best dive, the incredibly difficult but potentially high-scoring back two and a half somersault with two and a half twists, until last.

I put the scores out of my mind and vowed to do my best and be happy with the outcome, whatever it was. I kept telling myself, 'Do your best, that's all you can do. Don't worry about the score. Don't worry about Zhou messing up. Don't worry about medals. Relax ... relax ... enjoy this moment. Relax ... enjoy it ...' I felt terrific.

I dived.

I stayed underwater for as long as I could. 'Oh my God, oh my God!' I thought. 'That was a good dive. Could it win me bronze? Could it win me *silver*? No, Matthew, that is just too much to ask for.' I stayed under for what seemed ages, thinking that if my name was at the top of the leader board for this sixth dive, perhaps I *had* done enough to win silver. Then, lungs bursting, I kicked up to face the reality that surely waited — my name three or four from the top — that would dash my hopes. Already, my chronic self-doubt had taken over: was my entry really that good or did I over-cook it? Would my legs coming slightly apart from the twist to the pike, as they had, cost me points? Yet when I broke the water surface, the crowd was cheering. Chava was jumping up and down. Mum and Lachlan, high in the stands, were going bananas. I knew then that I'd done something special.

I swam to the side of the pool, climbed out and acknowledged the cheers from the grandstands. The entire crowd was going nuts, not just the Aussies. Even the Chinese, who must have been disappointed that their hero Zhou had come up short when it really mattered, cheered me. I waved, I raised my arms above my head, and I bowed deeply.

I looked up at the board where the judges posted their scores and I saw my name at the top. For my final dive, the judges had awarded me four perfect 10s, two 9.5s and a 9, giving me 112.10 points. I didn't know it at that moment, but this was the highest score for a 10 metre platform dive in the history of the Olympic Games. I then saw my accumulated points for all six dives: 537.95, and Zhou's tally: 533.15.

Right then it was the turn of the last finalist, the excellent Huo Liang, to dive. Weirdly, in my euphoric state, I was hoping he would do well. There was nothing I could do … I had done *my* job. I was oblivious to Huo's score and believed that if he produced his best dive he would pip both me and Zhou. In reality, if he had scored straight 10s and notched the maximum 114 points for that dive, he still would have been below my score. Huo muffed it anyway.

I had won the gold medal.

I couldn't believe it. Being the Olympic champion was my dream come true. I had been weeping ever since I thought I had won a silver medal, and now I'd learned I'd gone one better and I totally lost my shit. I howled with happiness.

I was mobbed. Chava, the realisation that he had coached a gold medal winner only now sinking in, bounced around like a delighted puppy. Like me, after my last dive he was convinced I had won silver. He had been yelling so excitedly that an official had told him to be quiet because Huo was still to dive. For the next five minutes, in all the chaos, he continued to believe I'd won silver. When people came running up to him in tears, he thought they were over-reacting. After all, a silver medal is fantastic, but it isn't gold. Then Jesus Mena – a Mexican diver Chava had coached to win bronze at the Seoul Olympics in 1988 and who is now chairman of the Technical Diving Committee of FINA – rushed up and hugged him. Mena said in Spanish, 'Congratulations on winning gold!'

Chava replied, 'No, we won silver'.

'Look up at the board,' said Mena.

Chava had trouble seeing the board clearly, but he knew immediately that I'd won because the longest name was on the top in the winner's position, and Matthew Mitcham is a long name compared with Chinese names.

'I reached the pinnacle of happiness that night. I don't think anything would beat that blissful feeling,' he later told me.

Finally he managed to fight his way through the throng to embrace me. Chava denies crying that night, but I have photographic evidence of him surreptitiously wiping away one little crystalline tear from his eye – maybe that's why he was having trouble seeing the scoreboard!

Alex Croak charged up and said, 'Oh my God, you've just won the bloody Olympics!' and hugged me. A Ukrainian coach presented me with a traditional doll. Mat Helm, who had won silver in the 2004 Olympics for the 10 metre platform and came sixth this time, said, 'Well done, you deserve it'. One German diver – straight, I hasten to add – came up close and whispered that he owed me a blow job, which cracked me up. You can see me laughing on the video.

People seemed to be genuinely glad that I won. Many appreciated what I'd gone through to arrive at this moment. Also, diving is a small sport and there's no room for enemies. No matter what country we are from, we are all mates. I've always had a good relationship with the divers and coaches from other teams. I've made an effort to learn a few words from every language and be personable. I smile at everyone.

Only the vanquished Chinese divers held back. They understood that anything less than winning every diving event was unacceptable to their coaches and administrators, and they may have been afraid of being punished. I did my doping test with Zhou and Huo, and they ignored me. It was very uncomfortable for us all.

When I stood on the medal podium, flanked by Zhou and third place-getter Gleb Galperin of Russia, I thought, 'It's all been worth it. All the shit. The sacrifices made by my mum and grandma, by Lachlan. Chava's dedication and belief in me. All my unhappiness when I was diving in Brisbane. The poverty and scrounging under seat cushions for money and the noodles and the baked beans. The endless train trips. The gruelling training. Getting clean'. If I hadn't battled my way through depression, self-harm and drugs, I simply would not have had the grit and determination to win a gold medal.

At this point, too, I remembered what the Diving Australia official said about me: 'If he ever makes it back on track we'll call it a miracle.' Well this *was* a miracle.

I lowered my head and an official placed the gold medal – it was much heavier than I expected it to be – around my neck, and I sang the Australian national anthem very loudly. I hugged Zhou and Gleb. I wanted to share the love. After all, we had all won Olympic medals.

People have asked me in the years since how I was able to produce an all-but-perfect dive when it mattered most, when other divers who were just as good as me failed in that 10 metre platform final. I'm sure that my cue words definitely played a part. What is undeniable, too, is that when I was up there on the platform waiting to dive, I *really was* enjoying myself. Chava says I'm a performer more than a competitor, and he is right. I am a show pony. I have been ever since I was spotted mucking around at a local pool that summer's day, which had started this whole thing. A lot of people have commented on how much they enjoyed and were excited by watching me, not just because of my diving but because of my interaction with the crowd and the cameras. I drew positive vibes from the goodwill of the crowd, and I wanted to show them and the world what I could do. The joy I obviously felt throughout that final was contagious. The crowd were infected by it and got behind me, and my smiling through what must have seemed a high-pressure situation made the judges, I suspect, favourably disposed toward me as well. That's my theory, at least.

My waterworks continued through the medal ceremony and for a good while after. I'm a massive cry baby. My face was scrunched into an ecstatic smile even while the tears flowed. Not a pretty sight. I was euphoric. I hugged Mum and gave her the flowers I'd been presented with, and I threw my arms around Lachlan. Kissing Lachlan on the cheek seemed the most natural thing in the world to do. As Lachlan laughed and said later, 'I'd have expected nothing less! After all, we had a lot to celebrate'. The cameras of TV networks all over the world caught me kissing Lachlan on the cheek. All but the major American network NBC – whose commentator had apparently shrieked, 'Did I just see Matthew Mitcham *kiss* that guy!' – mentioned that I was gay and ran footage of the kiss. It was said that our grandstand smooch was one of the iconic moments of the Beijing Games.

After the doping tests, I was shoved in front of the accredited media and interviewed. It was mentioned that I was Australia's first male Olympic gold medal-winning diver since Dick Eve in 1924. I rambled incoherently to the clamouring reporters: 'This is absolutely surreal. I never thought that this would be possible. I wasn't even sure of my medal chances at all, then I saw my last dive and thought that's it, it's a silver medal, and I was so happy.' To another reporter who asked how I was feeling, I sobbed, 'It's going to take a while to sink in. My cheeks hurt from smiling. My face hurts from the chlorine. My legs are sore from jumping up and down. I'm in pain and I'm tired, but I'm so happy'. One interview was in French, and although I practically speak the language fluently, it was like watching Britney Spears go through that head-shaving phase: a total train wreck. I couldn't think straight in English let alone a second language. I like to think I'm an articulate person, but all that came out was the same set of clichés you might expect to hear during a post-footy-game interview.

Then I was escorted across the road to do non-accredited media, and that was what I imagine a rugby scrum would be like, a battery of cameras and lights and reporters shouting questions at me in many languages. It was a bit scary. I said little, smiled a lot and showed off my medal. The cameras flashed and popped, as the photographers kept shouting at me, 'Over here, Matthew!' I obliged and couldn't resist pulling some funny faces, so there I was, posing for posterity with my gold medal around my neck or clamped between my teeth – making that old joke of testing its authenticity – and I'm mugging like a lunatic.

By the time I arrived back at the Olympic Village, it was after midnight. I went to the food hall and ate. I was starving. Everywhere athletes were celebrating their own victories. Some were drinking wine, and I wanted to join them, but thought better of it.

I had to be up and about at 5am for yum cha and more media duties and to sign some Olympic memorabilia near the Australian headquarters. That's where I met fellow gold medallists pole vaulter Steve Hooker and kayaker Ken Wallace for the first time. Steve and I have hung out quite a bit since. We caught up in Cologne when I attended the Gay Games in 2009 and he was training in the city at the same time.

Back home in Australia, my win was front page news. 'Perfect Dive Seizes Crown', 'Mitcham Foils Chinese Diving Clean Sweep', 'Golden Finale', 'Mitcham's Glory Dive', 'Golden Twist', 'Mitcham's Stunning Final Dive Leaves China Shattered', 'Aussie's Perfect Plunge!'. I was even on the front page of the major Chinese daily newspaper, quite a generous gesture from the parochial Chinese press, who had enormous trouble coming to terms with my preventing their hopes of a Chinese diving clean sweep.

I really appreciated the article written by American journalist Jim Buzinski which appeared on Outsports.com right after I won my gold medal:

Matthew Mitcham made me cry.

It takes a lot for me to weep while watching sports, but that's how moving his gold-medal diving performance was Saturday in Beijing …

By winning the gold medal in the men's 10 metre platform diving, Mitcham struck a golden blow for gay people everywhere who've been told they're flawed or not good enough, especially in the athletic arena. For all the gay men who have been called weak, sissies, pansies, too emotional, not tough enough to compete in sports, that final dive was for you. Mitcham helped to shatter those stereotypes and brought me to tears thinking about what was possible …

He has understandably said that he does not want to be known as the 'gay diver'. 'Being gay and diving are completely separate parts of my life,' he told journalists after winning the gold. 'I'm happy with myself the way I am.'

Of course, that is the attitude he should take, but he has become a role model for gays everywhere, whether active in sports or not, simply by being the way he is. We celebrate Mitcham for his courage off the platform and his talent on it ...

After the Olympics, I holidayed in Rome with Lachlan and our friend Jonathan from the Watsons Bay days. I entrusted Chava with my gold medal to bring back home. When he asked me where I was going to keep it when I returned to Australia, I said, 'Safe in my heart'.

Jonathan, who lives in the cobblestoned Trastevere district in the centre of Rome, one of the oldest and most romantic parts of the city, held a gold party in my honour. Guests had to wear a glistening gold outfit and some had gold body paint. There were gold balloons.

That was an idyllic month, hanging out with Lachlan and Jonathan and our friends in Trastevere. Sometimes in life there are wonderful times, and that Roman holiday, basking in my Beijing Games success and the bright future that awaited me, was pure gold.

It was while we were in Rome that I became aware of a controversy that had exploded all over NBC when gay rights groups accused the American broadcast network of homophobia for not running footage of Lachlan's and my kiss or even mentioning that I was gay. NBC apologised, however the LGBT – the gay, lesbian, bisexual and transgender – community were not placated, and several journalists hit back at NBC. They said it smacked of censorship that while NBC had extensively covered the personal lives of heterosexual athletes, including their relationships and tortured love affairs, they hadn't mentioned that Lachlan was in Beijing with me. The network issued an apology.

I didn't respond to NBC or anyone else. It wasn't my fight. If NBC had been horrified by a gay kiss between two men who loved each other very much, then that was their problem. I didn't care. I was on holidays in beautiful Rome and I had won a gold medal!

10

fame games

arrived home in late September 2008, tanned and sufficiently unwound after my month in Rome. I quickly found that, as an Olympic champion, life for me was very different. After 20 years of anonymity, people now recognised me when I was out and about. A day or so after I was back in Sydney, I was walking down the street, and as two girls passed by, I heard one say to the other, 'That was Matthew Mitcham, the diver!' I blushed. I was genuinely shocked.

I was surprised to learn that my win had resonated with so many. People wanted to tell me how much it meant to them. They confided to me that they would remember all their life what they had been doing when they saw me win the gold medal. Several said they had been in a pub, in Australia or overseas somewhere, and demanded that the television be changed over to the diving. Invariably, everybody else in the pub started to get behind me, irrespective of their own nationalities. When I won, there were hundreds of drunk people all over the world, chinking their pints together to celebrate the victory of someone they didn't know from a bar of soap. One person told me he was in his car on the way to work when the news came on the car radio, and he turned right around and treated himself to a sickie, so he could go home and watch the replays on TV (any excuse will do). It was quite weird. My great aunty was on a bus tour of China during the Olympics, when the tour guide announced, 'For any Australians on board, here is some good news. An Aussie has just won diving gold'.

My great aunt piped up, 'That wouldn't be Matthew Mitcham, would it?'

'It certainly is,' the guide replied.

Everybody burst into applause and cheered. They were happy anyway that an Australian had won gold, but they let out an extra roar when they found out that it was her great nephew.

I felt as if I had a big, flashing neon arrow hovering above my head. Every time I ventured out, alone or with Lachlan, I would see people do the double-take-and-whisper. But I knew (or at least assumed) that nothing nasty was being whispered, because I would be congratulated or complimented by at least three or four complete strangers whenever I left the house!

The more media interviews I did, the more I was recognised by people, especially in the gay community. I value my privacy, and no longer being Mr Anonymous took quite a bit of getting used to. While I loved that my achievement at the Olympics had affected and influenced people, it had its drawbacks, too, because sometimes I just wanted to go out and relax and have fun. A lot of people wanted to hear my opinion on gay rights. I have views, but I'm not an activist or a politician. I'm an athlete, just doing what I'm good at. Thank goodness the people who came up to talk to me were always polite, and it was never a chore to stay and chat.

Mum told me that a day or two after she returned to Australia after the Olympic final she was working as a barista in a café when a customer who worked for a high-end recruitment company brought a colleague down and insisted on introducing her to Mum, saying, 'You have to meet Vivienne Mitcham! She's the golden mum I told you about! Matthew Mitcham's mother!'

The other woman was almost hyperventilating, 'Oh my God! Oh my God! Vivienne, I watched your son on TV and ran straight to the bedroom and woke my husband, and said, "You're never going to believe this. Matthew Mitcham beat the Chinese in the 10 metre platform final!"'

I now had 30,000 friends on Facebook, and my page was inundated with messages, mostly congratulations, interspersed with dozens of marriage proposals, and a butt-load of suggestive messages that make you wonder whether courtship and subtlety are dying arts. Also waiting for me were more than 1500 emails saying well done. I had Facebook messages and emails from England, the United States, Italy and even China, where I'd been on the front page of the *China Daily*'s Olympic souvenir lift-out.

With the best of intentions, I started replying to the well-wishers. I felt so guilty for not getting around to reading and responding to about a thousand of those emails. It's not that I wasn't grateful; I just couldn't discipline myself to sit still long enough. So to all those who emailed me in August 2008, this is my Reply All: 'Thanks, Dollface xx'. If there were 25 hours in a day, I would love nothing more than to write to everyone who takes the time to write to me, but like my favourite air hostess, Pam Ann, I'm 'so very busy'.

I hoped that if people liked me they'd like my sport, and that was good for the future of diving in Australia. People kept telling me that when they watched me in the 2008 Olympic final, for them diving ceased to be a minor sport in which they could marvel dispassionately for a moment or two at the grace of the divers. In Beijing, as they barracked for me to come from behind and win, they could involve themselves in the sport for the first time with passion and pride.

While I tried to be a good role model in public, I had an inkling that there were some in the diving community who did not think I was good for diving, who were not comfortable with a gay, irreverent, face-pulling guy who trained out of Sydney being the highest-profile diver in Australia. I don't remember Hui congratulating me on my gold medal. That was OK. I understood. I've often wondered how Hui felt when I won in Beijing. Was he happy for me? However he felt about me, I still feel unhappy with myself for the trouble I caused Hui. In late 2008, admired and respected and clutching my new gold medal, it seemed to me that those days diving in Brisbane when I was unhappy, depressed and brattish were an age ago.

One of the perks of winning Olympic gold for Australia is having thousands of people lick and stick your face wherever they like. I was back in Australia only a couple of days when Australia Post released a set of commemorative postage stamps featuring my winning smile. Letters started flying in thick and fast, simply because people enjoyed the novelty of sending Matthew Mitcham a letter with a Matthew Mitcham postage stamp. It made checking the letterbox fun. Sarina Bratton, my friend and employer at Orion cruises, bought a whole sheet of stamps, framed it and presented it to me as a gift.

Poor Lachlan. After Beijing and Rome, he was looking forward to us having some quiet time together at home,

181

enjoying each other's company and blocking out the world for a while. Not a hope in hell. The Facebook and email deluge and the stamp issue were just the tip of the iceberg, as offers, invitations and proposals rained down on me for the rest of 2008. Lachlan struggled a little having to share me, and such a proud and private man was never going to be content with being known as Matthew Mitcham's boyfriend. In time, Lachlan came to accept the fuss as an inevitable by-product of my Beijing success; and after a bit, without embracing it, he was able to take the attention in his stride, just as I was. He even learned to laugh about it. Our relationship was secure.

All the compliments and positive feedback I got from strangers was addictive, for want of a better word. Having a bountiful supply of esteem-boosting material at my disposal for the first time in my entire life was incredibly seductive. I thank Lachlan, and Chava, Alex Croak and my great friend Alexis Paszek for keeping me grounded at this heady time. A little adulation was never going to change me drastically, I like to think, but these true friends would not tolerate any diva behaviour and had no issue with knocking me down a peg to ensure my head stayed the same size. When it was just us hanging out together, Lexi would say jokingly, 'Don't you know who I am? I'm Matt Mitcham's best friend!' and Lachlan would go, 'Don't you know who I am? I'm Matt

Mitcham's boyfriend!' (If I tried the same joke, they would *not* let me get away with it!)

After the Olympics, I was invited to appear on television shows and front up at awards nights and gala dinners, which required me to dress up to the nines. This was a problem because, while I had a gold medal, I had little money and the only clothes in my wardrobe were the same ones that had been there for years: $15 t-shirts, $30 jeans and $20 shoes. Among my favourite jeans are two pairs I've had since I was 14. They still fit, but after ten years of washing, the black jeans are now bluish-grey and the navy ones now pale blue. They still look all right, though: one time a high school girl I train with said, 'Cool jeans! Are they acid-wash?' She looked confused when I said 'No'.

I would have just worn my medal everywhere, but unfortunately it's not big enough to cover my junk. A friend with contacts at Versace and Armani told them I needed some good clothes, and they invited me in for fittings. Soon I had enough suits and shirts to mix and match indefinitely, all at no cost. I have worn those same clothes in various combinations ever since to events.

While juggling my personal appearances and other newfound commitments and responsibilities, I was back in training for the 2009 diving season, including the Australian National Championships in April, and the usual international

FINA events, all leading up to the Commonwealth Games in Delhi in 2010. I was once more doing 30 hours of diving a week, in 11 sessions with Chava. It wasn't easy telling him that I couldn't make training because I had to meet a sponsor or be on a TV show. I did not return to work at Orion, but most weeks I would do a speaking engagement for NSWIS, and requests were coming in from other organisations as well.

I was named the *Age* and *Sydney Morning Herald*'s 2008 Australian Sports Performer of the Year. I was also the co-winner, with pole vaulter Steve Hooker, of the Sport Australia Hall of Fame's 2008 Don Award, named after Sir Donald Bradman, 'for the athlete who most inspired the nation' and upheld Sir Donald's traits of 'sportsmanship, courage, dignity, integrity and modesty'. The Hall of Fame chairman was America's Cup-winning yachtsman John Bertrand. In announcing my and Steve's joint win, he said, 'There are aspects of both performances that captured people's imagination and showed young athletes around the country what you can achieve'. The other contenders for the Don were my friend swimmer Stephanie Rice, motorcycle champion Casey Stoner, hurdler Sally McLellan (now Sally Pearson), triathlete Emma Snowsill and cyclist Anna Meares. All except Casey were Olympians.

The *Courier-Mail* newspaper named me in their list of Queensland's '20 Toughest Athletes'. In response to readers who might have been surprised to see diving described as a tough sport, the paper wrote, 'Anyone who doubts the courage of divers never watched one of their daily training sessions as they slam into the water repeatedly, never mind how sore their hands, wrists and necks are. Plus, with Mitcham, the Brisbane-born Olympic champion has shown himself a tough enough personality to be one of Australia's very few openly gay elite athletes'.

Every athlete who wins gold at an Olympics receives an Order of Australia Medal, and in the 2009 honours list I was excited to be awarded mine. I've never received the actual medal, though, because every time I've been invited to go and receive it, I've always had a competition on overseas so I've had to politely decline. It's happened so many times, I think they've stopped sending me the letters inviting me! At first I used the little acronym, OAM, a lot but I have this tendency to always compare myself to other people, and I could only think about all the other, higher titles, like AM and AC, that other people have earned.

I remembered this episode of *Frasier* I'd seen in which Frasier and Niles accidentally receive the mail of somebody who lives in their building, and it includes a membership for a very exclusive health spa that they hadn't been invited to. So they pretend to be this person and his guest and go to the health spa – but when they find out that the membership only gets them into the lowest level, the exclusive membership they had envied doesn't seem good enough for them any more: they sneak through a door into the next, more luxurious section; and then they want to know what the next, more exclusive section is like, so they sneak into that. Not long after sneaking their way into this stunningly opulent room, they see another door. They just can't help themselves, and they go through – but it opens out into the back alley of the health spa, a dirty, seedy back alley.

It can become a bit ridiculous always looking up the ladder at the people on the rungs above, feeling less than them and aspiring to be like them. When I realised that, I calmed down a bit about using OAM after my name all the time. I began to appreciate the honour more for what it is: a recognition of my 'service to Sport as a Gold Medallist at the Beijing 2008 Olympic Games'.

To help me cope with all the requests that were coming in for appearances, I got a manager: David Flaskas, the head of Grand Slam International, which handled Ian Thorpe. Grand Slam had its work cut out. They found it was not easy attracting sponsors for an openly gay athlete. Many companies shy from controversy and don't want to alienate the market by associating their products with gay people. Some have no faith in the pink dollar. Grand Slam did their best to make me as mainstream as possible. Perhaps the Global Financial Crisis, which had just hit and was making companies reluctant to splash around their money, had something to do with it, too. Around December 2008, though, Telstra sponsored me to make appearances for them when they opened stores and launched products.

I tried hard and did all that David asked of me. I said yes to any number of media interviews – big city tabloids and broadsheets, local papers, glossy magazines, gay publications – and, now I had the swish clothes to wear, public appearances. I was grateful to the press for the respectful way they had treated me in the past; I was always comfortable being interviewed and never reticent to air my beliefs and be open about being gay. I hoped that if I was always accommodating and honest, there would never be a reason for the media to turn against me as it had against some high-profile acquaintances.

The problem that I faced was that I was a diver, not a natural celebrity. I was a dorky kid who pulled off something special on a grand stage. Being nice to people was well and good, and I found it easy to do, but celebrity didn't come easily to me. I felt under immense pressure being in the media and social spotlight, and felt terribly conflicted having to front for appearance after appearance when I would preferred to have been training with Chava or having fun with Lachlan and our friends.

One TV appearance I definitely did enjoy was when I was a guest on *The Pam Ann Show* on Foxtel's Comedy Channel. Pam is the beehive-haired alter ego of comedienne Caroline Reid, and she is a very funny lady with a big gay following. She is also not afraid to push the envelope, so when I was her guest I joined in the naughty spirit of the occasion. She introduced me to the studio audience: 'Ladies and gentlemen, it's time to limber up and wax every hair on your body ... Olympic gold medal winner Matthew Mitcham!'

I emerged from backstage wearing my green and gold Australian training gear and, to the applause of the crowd, did a standing back flip. The set comprised a structure like an Olympic medal winner's dais on which stood two buffed guys wearing only skimpy cossies, and Pam's circular fur-covered bed. Pam and I reclined on the bed, and she asked if I could place the medal around her neck. I took it from my pocket and put it on her, after a fair bit of trouble fitting it over her huge hair. She asked me if I had a mantra before I dived, and I said I did: 'Shit ... fuck ... shit ... don't fuck it up!' I then raved on about how the Chinese divers' swimming costumes have a strip of see-through mesh up the crack so when they bend over 'it's like, "Hello boys! Here's my Olympic ring!"' Bit rude, sure, but I was in my element and enjoying myself enormously.

At Pam's invitation, I flipped over onto my back and pulled my legs up over my head demonstrating my tight pike.

I stuck my face out from between my legs and quipped for all to hear, 'Lachlan likes this one!' Pam and the audience went crazy and she congratulated me on being so secure in my sexuality. A lot of gold medal winners appear on a lot of TV talk shows, but I don't think any have ever put on a show quite like that.

Back in serious mode, my manager David and I went to the cossie maker Aussie Bum to work out a sponsorship deal with them. Aussie Bum seemed a good fit for me, as not only do they make swimwear, but gay guys are a big part of their market. They offered me $100,000 over four years leading into the London Olympics. For $25,000 a year, they wanted me to work in their office for around five hours a day Monday to Friday gaining experience in the business and possibly launching a signature line. That was not realistic and certainly not what I was looking for. I didn't want a five-days-a-week job because I had to dive every day, and just squeezing in a few hours a day with Sarina Bratton at Orion had seriously worn me out. Happily, another swimsuit manufacturer, Funky Trunks, got behind me, so to speak. For Foxtel I appeared in my first ever TV ad. I was psyched to be in it, because it was a very schmick ad. It was a shot of me doing a dive, but in reverse, starting with me underwater, and it was in super slow-mo. I liked being associated with something so aesthetic and tasteful, and to have people come up to me and say they noticed it.

As well as Funky Trunks, Foxtel and Telstra, I have been supported by CAA, Hot Tuna, Coles and ProMax Nutrition. I certainly haven't been able to live an extravagant life on my sponsorship dollars, but added together, these sponsorships have meant that since the Beijing Olympics I have been able to make training my main job.

The then-Federal Health Minister Nicola Roxon made me an Australian Men's Health Youth Ambassador. In that role, I am on call to speak to sports clubs, community groups, organisations, companies, councils, universities and industry bodies. I was awarded the role after some controversy, when one of the first-appointed ambassadors, Lone Fathers Association president Barry Williams, was sacked. He had made the unfortunate – and, to me, astonishing – public pronouncement that being gay was a 'gender disorientation pathology' that was a symptom of personality disorder and sexual abuse. I have a theory that my appointment may have been an attempt by the government to make amends to the gay community. I was also made an ambassador for the Pacific Friends of the Global Fund, which cares for those in Pacific regions with malaria, tuberculosis and HIV–AIDS.

In 2009, I was appointed Chief of Parade of the Sydney Gay and Lesbian Mardi Gras in March. My role was to hold court on a float at the head of the big parade that wends its way from the Sydney CBD to Paddington.

We made a float from an old ute and put a stage on the back, on which I waved at the crowd and danced as huge speakers blasted out gold-themed songs: 'Black and Gold' by Sam Sparro and Freda Payne's 'Band of Gold'. Bringing up the rear behind the ute were seven boys dancing in rainbow-hued Speedos. Shane, who is a close friend of Lexi and mine, was in that group, along with some of our other friends. Then came Lachlan and our friend Jonathan, who we stayed with in Rome after the Olympics, along with three other guys; all five of them had large inflated tyres representing the Olympic rings. Next were seven friends who played the Olympic judges, dressed in white, each one holding up a score for my gold medal-winning dive at Beijing. The last row was a dancing gold-clad army of family and friends and supporters, including drag queen and comedian Joyce Maynge and Lexi, who was wearing a little beaded bra and tiny little mini skirt and massive high heels, all gold.

I was stoked to be asked; it's about the greatest honour one can be bestowed in the gay community. I believe the most positive thing I can do for gay people is not to be a hardline, humourless activist, but simply to live my life as a decent, caring and responsible human being first, and sportsman second. The fact that I am gay is incidental.

11

up and up

I began 2009 diving better than ever. In late January I scored a personal best of 541.70 to win the open platform at the Diving Queensland event, a qualifier for the Australian titles in Brisbane. I debuted a new dive, a complex back three and a half somersault pike that pushed my points skywards. Because of the physical difficulty of the dive, it had taken me about six months to build up the speed and strength to be able to do it in competition.

Then at the national titles in Brisbane in March, I notched a new personal best of 543 points in the 10 metre platform. For my third dive, an inward three and a half somersault, six of the seven judges awarded me a perfect 10. I also won the 1 metre springboard and the 3 metre synchro, in which I teamed with Grant Nel. Interviewed after the 10 metre event, I said, 'After Beijing, I've struggled at times with the pressure of expectation and I've been nervous about competing, but thankfully I haven't suffered what I call mental brain farts. That's when your brain just shuts down on the board'.

I believed that I was on track for wins at the FINA Diving World Series in Doha (Qatar) and Changzhou, China, in March, and the World Championships in Rome in July. None of that happened. In Doha, I was pipped for first place by my Beijing rival Zhou Luxin in the 10 metre platform, and came sixth in the 3 metre. In Changzhou, I placed sixth in the 10 metre platform and fourth in the 3 metre springboard. In Rome I did badly. I came fourth in the 10 metre, third in the 1 metre, ninth in the 3 metre, and 14th in the 3 metre synchro.

I was devastated by these results. The only solace was that I had done better than expected in the 1 metre event, given that I was the only one competing who was not a springboard specialist. My failure in the 10 metre platform event really tore me up because it was my pet event, my Olympic gold medal-winning event. In it, I was outscored by Briton Tom Daley, who came first, and my perennial rivals Zhou Luxin and Qiu Bo of China.

Even though I hadn't taken high school too seriously, deep down I was still that kid who had memorised facts out of the *World Book Encyclopedia*. I had always wanted to study at university. The degree I wanted to do, a combined bachelor of arts and science, was four years long. If I waited until I retired from diving, which could potentially be at 28, I wouldn't finish until I was 32, and then by the time I did a post-grad, I would be 37 before I could really start a career. I thought it would be better to start chipping away at a degree now, while I was still diving. Alex Croak, my friend from training who I had always looked up to, was managing to study full-time at the University of Sydney (not to mention maintaining a Distinction average) on top of all her diving commitments. So I figured I should be able to fit in part-time study.

In mid-2009, I started studying at the University of Sydney on a sports scholarship. Arts and science was the natural choice for me, because in high school my best two subjects were science and languages. I have loved science ever since I was a kid because most of the time the answer is either right or wrong; there is no subjectivity to it, as there is in English, which I was terrible at in school. Learning languages involves some subjectivity, but at high school it had largely been a matter of whether a translation was right or wrong.

I enrolled in a course in molecular biology and genetics. Because of the World Championships in Rome, I started the semester six weeks behind everyone else, so I spent the whole semester playing catch-up. Everybody else learnt the course in a sequential order, while I was learning things in the reverse order. I didn't realise how all these seemingly unrelated bits of information fitted together until about four weeks before the end of semester. Once I did piece it all together, I absolutely loved that subject and found it fascinating. I missed out on some marks because we were meant to be present for all the labs and I had to go away to compete. Despite all that, I still got a good grade, a credit.

The difficulty of juggling labs with travelling for competition was one of the reasons I ended up switching to Spanish and French. The other was that I tried to do calculus as a summer school subject so that I could do higher sciences the following year, but I failed it epically. I knew that while I was still diving, I needed to do courses that I would find easier. I like languages because I'm a very social butterfly: the more languages I can speak, the larger the population that I can be social with. I already had some French from high school, and from training with Chava I was picking up a lot of Spanish, which has similarities to French. Since I started learning, Chava will pick certain days to coach me only in Spanish; and when we're around other people and need to say something confidential, we can revert to Spanish.

Towards the end of 2009, I was invited to appear on the second season of Rexona's *Australia's Greatest Athlete* television series. The concept is that eight elite sportsmen compete in a variety of athletic challenges, including mini ironman,

25 metre swim, oztag (noncontact rugby league), soccer, jet skiing, a 40 metre running sprint, rock climbing, bench pressing, kayaking and driving a V8 buggy. I would be up against rugby league stars Wendell Sailor and Billy Slater, ironman Shannon Eckstein, rugby union's James O'Connor, racing car driver Craig Lowndes, Jason Culina the soccer player and AFL's Cameron Ling. At the end, the athlete with the highest combined score would be named Australia's greatest athlete. The different challenges would be filmed at Couran Cove Island Resort on South Stradbroke Island. I was happy to participate because if I won, the prize money of $10,000 would be donated to a charity of my choice.

I have never been much of a one for ball sports, and endurance sports are definitely not my cup of tea, so that put me at a disadvantage in most of the events, and overall I finished second last. In the multi-sport challenge event, the tyre I had to drag through the sand weighed half my body weight! I had gone into the show telling myself I didn't have to win and shouldn't blow it up in my mind to be too much of a big thing, but I did feel very self-conscious. I did my best to try and put on a brave face and keep it as light-hearted as possible – but actually I took it pretty seriously while trying not to.

The boys got to have a good laugh when we had to jet ski around an obstacle course. I'd never been on a jet ski before, and they only gave us one practice run. I didn't know how to steer the thing, so I thought that rather than trying to weave through the buoys, it would be a smarter idea for me to go straight up one side, do a big loop at the end and come down the other side and just accept the two-second penalty for not going around each buoy. I still took three times as long to do the course as the next slowest guy, and that was without having any of the penalties added! Even I was able to have a good laugh about that challenge, because I was just *so* atrociously bad at it.

When Lady Gaga came to Sydney to play the Sydney Entertainment Centre early in 2010, it was a big gay event. I made a unicorn horn out of a styrofoam cone and wrapped gold ribbon around it and wore it on my head. I bought a white feather boa from a two-dollar shop and stuck it to the back of the horn to be my mane. After plucking a few feathers from the boa and gluing them to my snail trail, aka treasure trail (the hair that runs down from the belly button), I attached the rest of the boa to my white pants to be the unicorn's tail. It was always going to be an out-there concert and I wanted to stand out. I wanted to be gay and proud. I love Lady Gaga and was so keen to meet her. I like what she stands for, as she's such an outspoken advocate for gay rights. I enjoy her acoustic recordings, where it's raw and you hear just her theatrical voice and wonderfully melodic and complex keyboard playing, and you can tell that she was trained as a concert pianist.

I spent the week before the concert sending her messages on Facebook and Twitter telling her who I was and wondering if she'd like to see my gold medal. I never got a response from her, obviously, because she's a superstar – but friends, and people on Twitter too, encouraged me to keep trying. I reckon I could have got through the wall of security to have an audience with Lady Gaga, but when it came to the crunch on the night at the concert I was too self-conscious to approach the guards backstage and try to gain admission to her inner sanctum. I thought, if I was in her position and everyone was trying to get backstage to see me, I would really want some privacy, plus who was I to think that the rules should be broken for me?

After my win at Beijing, without really trying to attract a following, just by being who I am, gay people from Australia and all over the world sensed a kindred spirit. Many contacted me saying I was making life easier for them. I was featured in gay magazines, often on the cover. I wanted to give back to the gay community for all the support they had given me, so I never said no when asked to attend a gay event, so long as I wasn't expected to stand on a pulpit and be a windbag. I did a couple of 21 Down events for young gay, lesbian, bi- or whatever sexuality kids aged up to 21. I handed out ribbons on World AIDS Day and attended the Gay Games in Cologne.

Everywhere I went, people would tell me how surprised they were that all the media attention after my gold medal win hadn't changed me. They commented on how down-to-earth I was, happy-go-lucky, comfortable in my own skin.

But appearances can be deceiving.

12

beneath the surface

So there I was ... I had a gold medal, won in spectacular fashion; I was one of the most feted and honoured athletes in Australia. I was on TV and had sponsors and ambassadorships. I now had 45,000 Facebook friends. I inspired gay people; they constantly told me so. Life with Lachlan had settled down again, and we were happy together. Chava had mapped out a schedule for me that included FINA events and the Australian Nationals, the Delhi Commonwealth Games in 2010 and the London Olympics in 2012, which were going to be huge. To see me bounding around like a cute and excited puppy on TV talk shows and accepting my gongs in front of black tie audiences, I looked happy and contented. No one looking on would have guessed that my depression, inherent self-doubt and low self-esteem were finding ways to turn all of this good fortune into an overwhelming downer. Giving up antidepressants in 2007 turned out to be a mistake. I had really thought I was cured. After the Olympics, because I had no immediate goal, I slipped into old behaviours and ways of thinking.

I convinced myself that I was a sham. I came to believe that my Beijing win was a fluke. That unless I followed it up with more gold in London in 2012 I would be exposed as a flash in the pan. I went on the FINA website and took a look at the world rankings. Because I had only won one Grand Prix event (at Fort Lauderdale) and the Olympics, I hadn't accumulated enough points over the year to be ranked No.1 in the world. I was No.2. All the pride and joy from winning my Olympic gold medal instantly evaporated as I realised that I had still failed to achieve my childhood dream of becoming the best in the world at something. I felt like I still had everything to prove and my Beijing gold counted for nothing. I believed that people were only befriending me because I was an Olympic champion. I can see now that this was deeply ironic given that one of my motivations for being the best was to win friends, but lucid self-analysis was not one of my strong points at the time. I told myself that I had no right to win the Don Award, beating out those other *genuine* champions. Twenty people could say complimentary things about me, and one person something derogatory, and that was enough for me to disregard the praise and stew on the criticism.

I kept all of this to myself. Though I know that it is not true, I felt that it was a sign of weakness to have emotional problems and depression. I didn't want to be a complainer, I didn't want to seem ungrateful, and I didn't want to burden people with my problems.

When people noted my good fortune, I told them, 'I don't want to be famous. I don't want to be rich. I want only enough money to pay my bills. I want to be happy and continue diving'. That was true sometimes. Mostly it was a self-protection mechanism. I knew that everything would fall in a heap when I was exposed as a fake. Occasionally, in the cold light of day, I realised that my damaging ruminations were groundless, ridiculous even. But when I was down, I convinced myself that those beliefs were valid, and continued to undermine myself.

Worst of all, a year after the Beijing Games, what *was* true – and what was tearing me apart – was that my old addictions had reared up again. I was parading myself as a virtuous role model for young Australians, gay and straight, when I was again seeking relief in drugs and alcohol to cope with my self-doubt and all my new responsibilities and obligations.

I didn't dare tell Lachlan that I had fallen off the wagon. To keep it from him, I never used at home. I would do it in my car when I left in the morning, or I would find a bathroom somewhere. If I needed an excuse to get out of the house, I would volunteer to go down to the supermarket or run errands. I hid drugs in various places, including the case for my reading glasses, which I kept in my training bag. Lachlan would ask, 'Why are you taking your training bag to go shopping?' and I would tell him that I was just leaving it in my car for later. It was exhausting: my mind was in overdrive all the time, thinking about where my glasses case was and where I needed it to be for next time. Whenever Lachlan noticed I was withdrawn or cranky, I put it down to being tired from training and my public appearances.

I had never stopped having an addictive personality. I'd been addicted to encyclopedias, trampolining, diving, then alcohol and drugs, until I dragged myself away from them to get clean to dive. Then pursuing my Olympic dream and hard training had been my addiction and had satisfied my compulsive need to do things on an excessive scale. I have been told that if you quit drugs and booze cold turkey, as I did, without working out the reasons why you are an addict in the first place, then the addiction manifests in another area. My addiction to diving and training had lasted until the Olympics. After the Olympics, when I had achieved my goal, life seemed a great anticlimax. Diving was no longer enough, and I returned to drugs and alcohol. I drank most days. I began using drugs around every second day, except when I was competing, when I didn't use at all so I didn't run the risk of being busted in a drug test.

I was using crystal methamphetamine, also known as ice, a potent and highly addictive synthetic drug. There are several ways to take crystal meth – I chose to smoke it like crack, in a pipe. I had dabbled in it in Brisbane but quit when I went to Sydney in early 2007. Catching the train to Olympic Park for training, I'd pass through Lidcombe Station, and on the wall there was a large graffiti recreation of the poster of the movie *Ice Age*. The words accompanying the graffiti read 'Crack Down', and there was also a picture of a glass pipe and a bong spray-painted around it – a reference to crystal meth, or ice. Every time I got to Lidcombe Station, even if I didn't look at the graffiti, I knew that it was there; and knowing that made me miss the drug. It was six months before I could pass that station without a pang. Then, in late 2009, I began using it again.

I knew what a dangerous drug crystal meth is. It is an amphetamine that releases dopamine into the body, revving up the brain and nervous system and giving a temporary but intense high. It can damage the brain, heart and kidneys, cause stroke and convulsions and insomnia, paranoia and violent behaviour. It can kill you. I didn't care. Taking it was something that I did to satisfy needs that I had to take my mind off things that were upsetting me, to make me feel better about myself.

In hindsight I can't believe how oblivious I was to the fact that I was using drugs to try to medicate my depression. I felt down, so I took uppers. Then I came down and felt even worse. So I took more uppers. I came down, felt worse, took more uppers ... and every time I did, it just perpetuated and reinforced the cycle. I knew it was a really short-term solution, but at the time I thought it was my most effective coping mechanism. Of course, I wasn't alleviating my depression; I was only making it worse.

It continues to amaze me that in the first half of 2010, even while I was knocking myself around, I enjoyed the best diving results of my life. There is no doubt that a driving factor in my success was my dismal fourth in the 10 metre platform event at the 2009 World Championships in Rome. That was such a crushing blow. I would try to redeem myself with a gold medal in the event at the Delhi Commonwealth Games.

At the Australian Nationals in January 2010 at my home pool, the Sydney Olympic Park Aquatic Centre, I placed first in the 1 metre, 10 metre and 10 metre synchro events, and second in the 3 metre and the 3 metre synchro. Then in Veracruz, Mexico, at the FINA World Series, I won silver in the 10 metre event. At the Canada Cup FINA Grand Prix in Montreal in May, China's Chen Aisen and I were going dive for dive throughout the 10 metre final. Not only did

I end up winning the final, I achieved a personal best score of 561. In the 3 metre synchro, I had to bail out of one of my dives because I thought I was going to hit my partner, Ethan Warren. For this dive, I had to start at the back end of the springboard, take a few steps and do a hurdle – that's when you raise one knee to a 90-degree angle and jump on the other leg before coming down on the end of the board on both feet and springing into the take-off. When you hurdle, you should land a couple of centimetres back from the end and right in the middle of the board. This time, I landed a couple of centimetres back from the end – but off to one side of the board. The springboard would propel me even further to that side – which was the side closest to Ethan. Afraid that I was going to hit him, I did a simpler dive so I could keep my eye on him and avoid collision, which meant we received no score. But we came back strongly on our last dive, which in most people's opinion was the synchro dive of the meet.

Next I competed in the 10 metre platform at the FINA World Cup in Changzhou, China, in July. My fierce rival Tom Daley of Great Britain did not compete – he remained at home perfecting his dives for the looming Commonwealth Games – and Beijing bronze medallist Gleb Galperin was also a no-show, but I was up against China's Huo Liang and Qiu Bo. In the final, I was running fourth after my first two dives, then scored 99 points with my third dive, a reverse three and a half somersault tuck, which drew 10s from all seven judges. Huo Liang overtook me with a brilliantly executed back three and a half somersault pike. Then in my last two dives, I surged ahead, scoring 97.20 in the fifth and 100.80 in my sixth, to give me a total of 562.80, eclipsing my personal best and putting me 7.40 points ahead of Huo Liang and 8.1 ahead of Qiu Bo. In fact, the top six finalists all scored higher than 500 points, which testifies to the quality of the competition.

Chava told me he knew I was relaxed and would do well in the World Cup when one of the other divers dropped a chamois and I clambered down off the platform and retrieved it for him with a cheery smile. Tightly wound, stressed-out competitors don't worry themselves with such niceties.

Afterwards, holding my gold medal tightly, I fronted the media and didn't try to conceal my excitement: 'Today was my lucky day! It was a very close competition, everyone was giving his best, and that pushed me to try my best, too. The standard was incredibly high. It's much harder to be the champion today than it was two years ago at the Beijing Olympics.'

My World Cup win in Changzhou was especially satisfying because, just as in Beijing, my victory prevented a Chinese clean sweep of the eight diving events. They won everything except the 10 metre platform. That I had again

208

deprived the Chinese of the glory they considered was rightfully theirs was too much for some of the local media representatives. At the press conference, they betrayed their disappointment and frustration. One interviewer made it sound as though I got lucky when I won in Beijing and now in Changzhou; it wasn't that I was better than the Chinese athletes, just that they made mistakes. I saw red. 'Oh,' I retorted in my most irony-laden voice, 'Forgive me … It was an accident. I didn't mean to win!' Irony doesn't always translate, and some of them actually believed I was apologising for winning.

The Chinese divers and coaches are generally friendly to me. Because of the bit of Mandarin I'd studied, I know a few funny sayings, such as 'Too fat' and 'I'm a stupid egg,' which makes them laugh. I think they also like me because I refer to all of them as *wǒ de hǎo péngyou*, 'my good friend'. They are not so cheery when I beat them. As being coached by Hui and the other Chinese coaches in Brisbane taught me, to the Chinese winning is everything.

After my FINA World Cup 10 metre platform win in Changzhou, FINA officially ranked me the number one 10 metre platform diver in the world. Perhaps, just perhaps – I allowed myself to think for a quick minute – I really did deserve my Olympic gold medal. The moment I learned of my top ranking was the first time I had felt a sense of achievement since Beijing. Chava was confident that I was on cue to win gold at the Commonwealth Games in Delhi in October.

My good results belied that I had constant severe back pain. I didn't know it then, but I was competing with two stress fractures in my lower spine, in my L4 and L5 vertebrae.

To the best of my knowledge, I damaged my spine at the World Cup in July, when I performed a back three and a half pike and hit the water with an arched back and really crunched it. I got treatment for it on the spot from a chiro and the massage therapist, who applied bright yellow strapping tape down my spine as a way of reminding me to brace and protect my lower back during the finals. It looked funny, competing with this bright yellow tape coming out the back of my green togs. I ended up doing really well in the finals, but my back was sore from then on.

There was no chance for me to rest, as just two weeks later I had to take part in the Commonwealth Games trials in Perth. I struggled but qualified. My mystery back pain was getting worse, and I was developing new injuries. One of my shoulders was sore, and my wrists were hurting from having dived from the 10 metre platform almost every day for a month. I desperately needed a break, but it was obvious that I was not going to get one. My training intensified.

In September, two weeks before I flew out to Delhi for the Commonwealth Games, came a real bombshell. I received a text message from my new manager, Robyn Watson of the Sports Group. Robyn's message read: 'Who is Greg Swadling?' When I read it, I had shivers up and down my spine.

'Oh my God,' I thought. 'Where has this come from?'

I called Robyn. 'Greg Swadling is my dad.'

This man, the father whom I had never met, had contacted Robyn and asked if she would put him in contact with me. She was calling me to get my OK or refusal. I was in shock. This was the *last* thing I expected. Apparently he had been trying to reach me for some months, since he had read a magazine article earlier that year in which I said I wouldn't mind meeting my father one day and catching up over a beer (low carb of course), just to find out what he was like. Apparently, in his attempts to be in touch, he'd hit problems, mostly because I had moved a couple of times, and I had left my former management company. So when he finally sleuthed out that Robyn was my new manager, he called her.

After I mulled it over and talked the ramifications through with Lachlan, I decided that I did want to see my father. He had left his mobile phone number with Robyn, and I called him. I was so curious to see what kind of a man he was, what he looked like, whether we shared traits. I was keen to know what was on his mind. He was visiting Sydney, and we arranged to have dinner the following evening at a Thai restaurant on Darling Street, Balmain, near where Lachlan and I now live. Lachlan's mum bought the two-bedroom apartment, and Lachlan and I pay rent to supplement her mortgage repayments. Lachlan's mum and her partner come up to Sydney from the Southern Highlands regularly, and they stay in the second bedroom. I am so grateful for her generosity, because we would surely be paying more rent if we were living elsewhere, and during times of financial hardship she has been lenient about us being a bit late with the rent or has offered to pay the water or gas bill.

The afternoon of my meeting with my dad, I was a mass of nerves. I was at training, standing up on the 10 metre platform, when all of a sudden it hit me like a sledgehammer to the chest that I was only hours away from coming face to face for the first time with my father, the man who had left Mum before I was born. All the questions I had wondered about him for 22 years came flooding back at once. Anxiety overwhelmed me, and I had a bit of a cry up on the 10 metre tower. I sat down in the middle of the platform so nobody could see me, because a man in a swimsuit, dripping wet and blubbering like a baby, is not a pretty sight. I pulled myself together and finished my training session.

I went and met him, and I am happy to say that this man

whose DNA I share proved to be one of most lovely, most grounded people I had ever met. I thought, 'This is weird! … I had never thought of myself as being lovely or grounded!' He was the same height as me, possibly a little smaller framed. He was handsome, with nice teeth, and spoke and carried himself well. He was obviously intelligent. Knowing that fathers pass their propensity for baldness to their sons, I could not have been more relieved to see that he had a full head of hair. My grandad and uncle on my mum's side are completely bald. My anxiety alleviated within moments of shaking his hand, and I felt comfortable with him. I sat down. He said, 'So, is there anything you want to ask me? I'm sure you've got lots of questions'.

This was my chance to ask him all those questions like 'What did you think when you found out Mum was pregnant?', 'Did you ever wonder about me?', 'Did you ever want to meet me?', 'Do your wife and kids know about me?', but it felt like a soppy B-grade American drama already, so I kept it practical. 'Any genetic predispositions I should worry about?'

That question floored him. I couldn't help it; I wanted to know. I needed to find out if there was a chance I'd turn into a fruit loop by age 25 or develop heart disease or cancer. He was seriously unprepared for that question and said he would have to go away and think about it.

He told me a bit about his life. In 1994, when I was six years old, he had married a woman named Yolande, and they had had a daughter, Mia, who is now 14, and son, Ky, now 10. They live at Coolum Beach, on the Sunshine Coast. He works as a sales manager at a pharmaceutical company, while Yolande, who used to be a biologist, is now a full-time mum. Greg is built like an endurance athlete — he's pretty small and weighs less than me — and competes in triathlons on the Sunshine Coast. He goes for several-kilometre bike rides or swims every morning, and plays soccer with his mates.

Obviously he had read that I was gay and so I talked to him about Lachlan. I didn't feel ill at ease divulging these personal matters to him at all, which was a measure of how comfortable I felt in his presence. He told me that he had watched me dive in Beijing and been proud, so lots of our chat that first night was about diving. I started to explain the technicalities of my sport and the scoring system and, as with most people, it all made his eyes cross and his head spin.

I didn't ask why he left Mum and me. I believe now that he was young and not ready for fatherhood and panicked and just took flight. I could understand that. Besides, he didn't completely abandon us in that he continued to support Mum financially and paid child support payments.

Dinner over, we got up to leave the restaurant, and he hugged me. I realised my dad did care about me.

Today we're friends. He and Yolande have since had me to stay at their home a few times. Their house is only about 200 metres from the beach, so it feels like a holiday every time I go up and stay with them. I spent Christmas 2010 with them and met Nanna and Poppy for the first time. When we met, Nanna cried, and said, 'You know you've been in our prayers often over the last 22 years'. Poppy sat down and did a crossword with me. I think we all were conscious of how emotionally intense the situation potentially was, so we tried to keep it light-hearted.

I soon noticed a similarity between Yolande and my mum. They both love animals. Mum always had chickens running through the house, and she always talked about how much she wanted a pig. Yolande rehabilitates injured or orphaned wildlife, like kangaroos and joeys and possums. Whenever the family is driving along and there's a dead marsupial by the side of the road they have to stop so she can check the pouch to see if there's a baby inside. She's always walking around with a sling bag, carrying around a baby kangaroo or possum everywhere she goes because she has to give them regular feedings.

Yolande – or Yollie, as I nicknamed her – was the most enthusiastic and most forthright about having me be part of the family. Right from the very beginning, the first time I went to stay with them, she said, 'Oh, it feels like our family is complete now' and 'It's really lovely to finally have you as part of the family'. Because Greg had never hidden my existence from her, I suppose I had been present as a concept throughout their entire relationship. In fact, Yollie has said it felt like something was missing. Perhaps connecting with me, it was as if a void was being filled: the empty consciousness of this extra child who had been there throughout their entire relationship was now filled in.

It took me a while to open up to the idea that she, Greg and Mia and Ky really wanted me to be a part of their family. I felt guilty at first about being embraced by them when I only see my half-brother Marcus – who I think of simply as my brother – about once a year and feel sad because he has missed out on a lot of family life. After Mum broke up with Marcus's dad, Marcus lived with me and Mum for a while, then for a few years he lived with his dad, and then for a few years he alternated between being looked after by Grandma and my auntie Jo. He went away to boarding school in Toowoomba, a couple of hours west of Brisbane, when he got an academic scholarship that pays for part of his fees; Grandad chips in the rest.

Another thing I felt a bit uncomfortable about at first was that after I had been up there a couple of times to visit, when they dropped me off at the airport, Yolande would cry or say, 'Love you'. I just wasn't used to that type of

216

affection from — well, anyone, I suppose. It was really hard for me to wrap my head around the concept that she would genuinely want me to be part of the family and that she cared about me like one of her own children even though biologically I wasn't hers. But the fact that she would cry and say 'Love you' helped me realise that this relationship is legitimate, it is real, and then I quickly became comfortable with it. Now I completely feel that Greg, Yolande and my half-siblings are part of my family, and that I'm part of their family as well.

13

breaking point

I arrived at the Commonwealth Games in Delhi in bad shape. A sign that I was not myself was when, just before Delhi, I was diving in a qualifying event in Perth and I miscued my take-off and one of my feet clipped the platform. When that happens, it completely disorientates you. By the time you realise your feet have hit, you've already done another one or one and a half somersaults. You try to orientate yourself, but you just have no idea where you are in the dive or where you are in space: you might think you're perfectly vertical when in fact you're about to hit the water flat on your stomach.

And when you do hit the water, there's a flash of white, and everything goes really silent for a second or two ... until you get this ringing in your ears, which lasts for another ten seconds or so. Then the pain sets in – the pain of smacking the water at 60 kilometres an hour. You go through a primal sort of personal inventory: you try to figure out what happened, whether you've got all your limbs, whether you hit your head or not. There are a few panicky moments where you try to judge if you are actually able to get to the surface of the water or you need help.

After it happened in Perth, when I hauled myself out of the pool, I was distraught. Chava came down and told me how important it was to shake off my fears and dive again immediately. I did so, and this time I dived flawlessly and was back on track for Delhi. I considered the mishap a wake-up call.

Delhi was awesome and like no place I had visited. The exotic sights, pungent smells, vibrant colours and ceaseless bustle impressed me every bit as much as the terrible poverty upset me. I was a little worried at the prospect of terrorism: there had been some terrible attacks in India in the recent past. In Mumbai in 2006, 209 were killed and more than 700 injured in a series of train bombings, and two years later in that city, terrorists struck and 172 died in bombings and shootings. (In Delhi itself in 2011, the year after the Commonwealth Games, 11 died when a bomb was exploded in the High Court building.) Happily, when the athletes of the Commonwealth gathered in Delhi, there were no incidents, possibly because the security was heavy – military men with rifles everywhere you looked, including on the athletes' buses and in the compounds – and it had been made clear that anyone caught trying to disrupt the Games would regret it.

I had heard that the organisers were suffering financial problems. If so, there was no sign of that at the pool, which was of the highest standard and a pleasure to dive in. And the vibe was a friendly one. I was in my element, chatting and laughing with the other athletes and the fans. As with every place I go to dive, I felt so privileged to be there.

Ethan Warren and I won silver in the 3 metre and 10 metre synchro events, and I took silver in the 1 metre springboard. In my pet event, the 10 metre platform, I faced Tom Daley, who had beaten me at the FINA World Championships in Rome. As Jessica Halloran, the journalist who broke the news that I am gay, wrote, the English teenager 'applied the blowtorch' to me in the final. Daley was awarded perfect 10s – along with gasps from the crowd – for his inward three and a half somersault. I scored my share of 10s and took the lead, on 275.30, in the third round. Daley, at 267.60, had ground to make up – but then I made a mess of the entry on my fourth dive. After that round, Daley was ahead of me, but only by .70 points. By the second last dive, I was trailing him by 1.75 points. It would all come down to the final dive. Daley scored 94.05 for his, a reverse three and a half somersault. The gold was within my reach when I launched myself from the platform for my last dive, a back three and a half somersault pike. I knew that I'd blown it as soon as I did it. My entry was clumsy, and I made a big splash. I finished with silver, on 509.15 points, 29.2 points behind Daley.

It was unlike me to falter when it mattered, and for that I blame my still undiagnosed stress fractures and a weakened mental state due to my secret personal excesses. Interviewed after the final, I was defiant. 'If this gives Tom a little bit of confidence, then good on him. But I am going to train that much harder to try and beat him in London. Absolutely, I can beat Tom. I did not even dive close to my best today. If I had, it would have been really exciting.' Tom's score was about 30 points below my personal best, and my score was about 50 below it. If I had dived to my potential, I could have smashed it − but I didn't. 'I am a little bit disappointed about my result,' I told the journalist.

A little bit! I was putting on a brave front. Besides, no one likes a cry baby, especially a cry baby who just won four silver medals, when most competitors don't win any. Still, the truth was that I was bitterly upset at being beaten in the 10 metre platform. I was proud to win silver in the other events, but not in my prize event. I felt like the biggest loser. I'd won an Olympic gold medal and a World Cup gold medal in the 10 metre platform dive, I was ranked No.1 in the world by FINA, and Commonwealth Games gold would have been the icing on the cake. To be beaten at Delhi laid me low. I expected more of myself, and because I was the current

Olympic champion I expected that Australia did too. I had let everyone down and I had let myself down. The defeat by Tom was yet another blow to my always shaky self-esteem, and after Delhi I moped around feeling worthless. My defiance dissipated as the old self-doubt gripped me.

I confess, I was also jealous. Everyone was crowing about Daley's achievement and that he was going to be the next big thing. I felt replaced. I found myself feeling inferior to Tom, who had now beaten me not only at the World Championships in Rome in 2009 but also at the Delhi Games. In spite of my FINA No.1 rating, could I really claim to be the world's best with Tom Daley on the scene?

There was no respite for me after the Commonwealth Games. Diving Australia decided to hold the 2011 National Championships in December 2010, when normally they wouldn't be staged until January. The diving season is usually six months long, but by this point, I had been hard at it for more than twelve months. I had started filming Rexona's *Australia's Greatest Athlete* late in 2009, then competed through to the World Championships in July. The season would normally have ended then, but it had been extended through to the Commonwealth Games trials and the Games themselves, and now the Nationals in Melbourne. I had overextended myself. And that's why I broke so badly.

My back pain had worsened throughout the Commonwealth Games, and at the Nationals I was in so much pain I couldn't sleep at night. In bed, I did everything possible to try to alleviate the pain. I lay on my side, on my back, this way and that. I slept with pillows under my stomach. I tried everything. Nothing helped. I popped Panadol and anti-inflammatories three times a day. Chava and I found a physio in Melbourne, who I saw every morning, and I got acupuncture to ease the muscle spasms around the still-undiagnosed stress fractures in my lower back. The physiotherapy and the needles gave me some relief – but not enough to be able to dive every day at the Nationals. Each day I arrived at the pool with my bag packed, ready for competition, and each time the physio would say, 'No, I don't think you're fit to compete'.

I was registered to compete in five events at the Nationals but I withdrew from all except the 10 metre. I had to compete in that in order to qualify for competition the following year. Somehow, despite the pain and the restriction caused by my back problem, I scored twenty-eight 10s across the prelims, semis and finals. Given the circumstances, I was satisfied with my scores. What concerned me was that normally I would feel that I performed six solid dives, but while some of my dives felt amazing and were rewarded with really high scores, there were some lacklustre ones, too.

Chava had been worried about me at the Nationals and while we were there had been on the phone to my doctor in Sydney, who organised for me to have a CT scan the day that I got back. The scan finally revealed the stress fractures. The doctor ordered me to take one month of bed rest, completely free of any physical activity, to give them a chance to mend. Then, while undergoing rehab on my back, I was to ease my way back into full activity over the next two months.

'Ideally,' the doctor said, 'I would like you to just starfish it in bed for a month.'

I said, 'But isn't that the kind of repetitive stress you want me avoiding?'

One corner of his mouth betrayed a tiny smirk, and he replied, 'You know what I mean'.

Starfishing it in bed (in the non-carnal sense of the term) was going to be boring, so I decided to learn a musical instrument. I picked the ukulele, because it seemed simple enough – it has only four strings, compared with the six strings on a guitar – plus everybody plays guitar, so I thought a ukulele would be cooler. I bought a $24 ukulele and taught myself by watching videos on YouTube. From there, I started teaching myself music theory.

I learned how to play old tunes – like 'Five Foot Two', which Mum used to play on the gramophone when I was a kid – but also contemporary songs. I sang along, and it helped me to relax, took my mind off my injury. I think creating any kind of music is really therapeutic. Now I take my ukulele everywhere I go. When I'm away competing, I play, and it makes the other divers happy, too. One night when I was competing in Canada, I had a dream in which the boy I was sharing a room with was in Katy Perry's film clip 'California Gurls'. I woke up, and he was awake too, so I told him about the dream, and I started playing that song for him on the ukulele. There we were, jetlagged, me playing 'California Gurls' at about 3am. on my ukulele, having a great time.

From playing the ukulele, I ended up teaching myself chords on the guitar and piano as well. Whenever I'm in Queensland, if my family can get Marcus to Brisbane from his boarding school in Toowoomba, he and I spend as much time together as we can, just hanging out. One time, I taught him how to play the duet 'Heart and Soul' on the piano. I also gave him my old ukulele and taught him a few chords so we could do a duet of Kylie Minogue's 'Can't Get You Out of My Head' – me on the piano, Marcus on the ukulele.

Two years after the Olympics, I was still recognised in the street, and this surprised me. Gay groups continued to invite me to support their activities, and often I was glad to.

People often ask me whether gay people should come out, and I say it must be up to the individual. Every person's situation is different. Some people who declare that they are homosexual may have to contend with religious, social, legal or political factors that could open them up to ostracism and persecution or even put them in harm's way. In many countries, it's illegal to be gay; in a handful, it can even mean the death penalty. In parts of Australia, until not all that very long ago, gay people were prosecuted. I'm incredibly grateful that, living in modern-day enlightened and sophisticated and tolerant Australia, I was able to be true to myself and suffer no criticism.

Being gay is not an abomination. Mum, for one, today feels really strongly that she should express and display her love for her gay son publicly. 'I wouldn't have him any other way,' she says.

I still don't consider myself an activist – just a guy who happens to be gay. The only time when I've got my hackles up and lashed out publicly at homophobic attitudes was when AFL player Jason Akermanis wrote in Melbourne's *Herald-Sun* newspaper that the world of AFL was not ready for openly gay players. Addressing rumours that some gay AFL players were about to declare their sexuality, he said that coming out was unnecessary and could break the fabric of clubs. He worried that gay men being in dressing rooms 'where nudity is an everyday part of our lives' could cause 'discomfort'. Akermanis cited the case of one gay footballer with whom he had played, saying that while he was a nice guy and a good player, when he walked into the dressing room the 10 other players walked out, clutching their towels to their nether regions. Akermanis felt uncomfortable, and he left too – although, on reflection, he thought that perhaps what he should have done was 'to sit down and talk with him in an attempt to understand his life'. How condescending. Although he supported any initiative that lessened public bias against gay people, such as IDAHO (International Day Against Homophobia), an AFL player being openly gay was just too big a burden for his teammates to bear.

To my mind, Akermanis's views were ignorant and just plain wrong. I thought he was making outrageous statements so he could stay in the headlines. I was so angry. I didn't want to be controversial, but I gave a magazine interview publicly rebutting what he said. Sport, like society, should accept gay people as human beings and afford them the same rights and respect as heterosexual people.

I was quite shocked when my friend and Olympic swimmer Stephanie Rice was accused of being homophobic. Steph's and my paths have crossed at events and functions over the past few years, and I have always found her a lovely girl, fun and clever. I can only assume she was experiencing a brain fart when, in September 2010, after the Australian Wallabies rugby union team defeated South Africa, Stephanie, who was going out with Australian player Quade Cooper, tweeted, presumably at the South Africans, 'Suck on that faggots ...' The out former rugby league champion Ian Roberts echoed the thoughts of many in the gay community when he called Steph an 'idiot'. I prefer to think that she just got carried away by the Wallabies' win and made a silly mistake. Certainly she has only ever been friendly and respectful to me and never once exhibited homophobia.

14

body blow

After the Nationals in December 2010, I took the rest of December and all of January off to try to get my stress fractures right. Then, in late February 2011, I went back into training, my long-term goal to successfully defend my Olympic gold medal at the London Games. The 10 metre platform would be my only event at the Games, and Chava and I set to work. After Beijing I had fallen into a slump, and Chava did not want this to happen again post-Delhi. He mapped out a program that would keep me focused and happy.

Chava wanted me to master the front four and a half tuck dive for the London Olympics – he thought I would need it in my armoury to win – but I resisted. I had had an accident doing the dive off the 3 metre board the previous year. I got lost mid-dive and landed with my feet instead of my head. Getting disoriented like that starts undermining your confidence about your safety. My reticence to do the dive had nothing to do with the physical challenge of it and everything to do with the fact that getting lost mid-dive had shaken up the foundations of my mental security. I've seen other boys get lost in that dive a few times, too, and it's just awful. Chava could see the prospect of having to do the dive was winding me up, so, reluctantly, he scrubbed it.

I threw myself into training. Simply put, I tried to do too much too soon, increasing my workload faster than my strength was able to regenerate.

I wouldn't know this for some months, but the premature and too-heavy workload saw me suffer a tendinopathy, a bunching of the fascia in my rectus abdominus (my six-pack), which is the precursor to an abdominal muscle tear. I thought this new pain in my abdomen was being caused by a simple strain and that I could tough it out. I went to Montreal to compete at the FINA Grand Prix event in April, because I needed to have one competition under my belt before the World Championships in Shanghai in July.

In Montreal, I defied the pain to dive, and every time I dived, in competition or practice, my muscle was taking more of a load so I further damaged my ab. I was strapped and was having my abdomen iced between dives, and was being treated by a physio and the massage therapist, yet the pain worsened through the three days of competition. Despite that, I made it through the preliminary event and the semi-final to qualify for the final. I wasn't strong enough to do my three and a half pike, so I did a back three and a half tuck, which I hadn't used in competition since 2008. I relearned the dive two days before the competition, and ended up taking gold with it in the final. I didn't even warm up before that final because I was hurting too much.

The abdominal muscle is so important in diving because every movement is ab intensive. Going from the jump off the board or platform into the position for the dive requires a lot of strength. This is especially true in the back three and a half pike, because you take off in an extended, arched position and use your abs to snap you into the tight pike as quickly as possible, effectively generating the momentum for the dive. And it's not just getting into the shape that you need your abs for, but also resisting the G-forces to hold that shape as you are spinning around. Diving with an injured ab is like a runner trying to run with a calf tear – the ab is as crucial as that.

Now, and much too late, I started to suspect that my ab had torn. Nevertheless I competed in the Grand Prix in Fort Lauderdale, Florida, the following week. Performing one dive in the semi-final, my ab failed me completely and I screamed in pain. By the way that my muscle swelled up afterwards, I knew my suspicion was correct and I had torn my abdominal muscle. I withdrew immediately from the Fort Lauderdale final.

Back home in Sydney, scans revealed a 2.5 centimetre by about 2 centimetre-long tear in the left side of my rectus abdominus. Such an injury normally takes a minimum of 10 weeks to heal, or may require surgery, but the World Championships in China were just eight weeks away and I was determined to fast-track my treatment so I could recover in time to compete there. Chava gave me four weeks of reduced training in which I did not dive and did no core training, just exercises to keep my legs and upper body strong and flexible. I wanted to avoid surgery, so I opted for a relatively new type of treatment, platelet-rich plasma (PRP) injections. They took some of my blood and spun it in a centrifuge to extract the plasma, which contains platelets. Then they ran an enzyme through the plasma to break up the platelets and free their growth factors. The plasma was then injected into my ab in the hope that the growth factors would help repair the tissue. I also did a daily session in a hyperbaric chamber to force extra oxygen into the abdominal tissues to speed up the recovery process.

All that done in the first month, my ab was feeling somewhat better and so I started training again for the World Cup in Shanghai. The best laid-plans … Just a week into full training, I reinjured my ab and had to withdraw from the World Championships. I was devastated. The year was fast becoming a disaster, and there was now a big question mark over whether I would be fit enough to qualify for the London Olympics, just 12 months away.

I had never had physical limitations before. In the past, if I put my mind to doing a dive, I could do it – maybe not straightaway, but I could eventually make it happen. Now my mind was fine but I could not allow my body to follow, because I knew I would risk further injuring myself. I was frustrated. I felt like I was driving and there were all these speed bumps forcing me to slow down; I hated not being able to go at my own pace.

I thought back to how proud I was to be ranked No.1 in world diving in 2010. That ranking had become my benchmark, the standard I measured myself against. So it was demotivating through 2011 to be injured and unable to achieve that benchmark. Along with that came self-loathing and self-defeating thoughts like 'You're a has-been' and 'You're never going to be that good again; you should just quit while you're ahead'. With great achievement comes perfectionism. Being unable to achieve world No.1 status since my injuries began, I felt like a failure.

Chava, who was as upset as I was, provided Diving Australia with the training plan he'd mapped out for me for the rest of the year. The program was written in consultation with my sports doctor, physiotherapist and strength-and-conditioning trainer to best ensure adequate recovery and rehabilitation of the muscle and prevent any reinjuries.

Chava hoped that Diving Australia would allow me a reduced schedule to assist my recovery, and he warned them of the good possibility I might not even be ready for the National Championships in December that year. But he was told in no uncertain terms that I would not be considered for the Olympics unless I dived well enough at the National Championships to meet National Squad selection criteria. I would also subsequently have to meet the selection criteria in the FINA Grand Prix in Rostock, Germany, in February 2012, the Diving World Cup in London the same month, the Diving Australia Olympic Games trials in Adelaide in early April, and the Grand Prix competitions in Montreal in May and in Fort Lauderdale a week later.

In my disappointment, I wondered if they were punishing me for past misdeeds. In fact, clearly they needed only fully fit divers at the Olympics, and if I wasn't fit, I may not be at my best at the London Games so it would be best to give my place to another diver who was. There is no room for sentiment in elite sport. Yet it didn't help my and Chava's dispositions when we read that the British diving officials were not making Tom Daley compete in all the lead-up events, so he would be daisy-fresh for the Olympics.

Once I would have reacted badly to Diving Australia's stance, maybe even thrown a tanty and walked away. Now I decided that I would do what they demanded, to prove to the world in London that my Beijing gold was not a fluke. To succeed in London in the 10 metre platform event I would need to be diving better than I ever had. My competition would be more intense, and I would be bearing the pressure of being the reigning Olympic champion.

Chava told me to put London out of my head for now and make getting in shape for the Australian National Championships in Adelaide – just six months away, in December – my No.1 priority. After that, I would take it event by event and hope I would do well, or at least not break down.

Chava altered my style to minimise the strain on my abdominals when I dived, and so ensured that I did not exacerbate the injury. Small things, like minutely readjusting my angle of entry into the water. I worked hard. I wanted to go to the London Olympics so very much.

But before anything, I had to say goodbye to drugs.

What I am revealing in this book, confessing to having been a drug user, will shock many. I know that, and there is nothing I can do, for people will react to my revelation as they see fit. I would not blame anyone for turning their back on me and calling me a sham. I *was* a sham. All I can do now is be honest. I am inspired by the example of Fergie, the singer with The Black Eyed Peas, who had a crystal meth addiction and aired her addiction publicly and has suffered no backlash. Andre Agassi, too. I hope my friends, fans and sponsors prove to be as forgiving as Fergie's and Andre's seem to be. I'm clean now. Perhaps others caught up in the despair and pain of drug addiction will read this and see that it is possible to beat it.

Late in 2010, after the Commonwealth Games, I had told Lachlan I was using drugs. I did so not because I wanted his help to stop, but in the hope that he would break up with me. My addiction had twisted my mind to the point where I wanted to sabotage the relationship. Instead of blaming my addiction for my unhappiness, I blamed my relationship with Lachlan, because it was an obstacle to my taking drugs.

Lachlan was shocked, angry and devastated. He had never dreamed I was using, though he had felt for some time that there was *something* wrong, because it seemed that I had drawn a net around myself; for the first time since we'd met, he'd been finding it hard to communicate with me.

One of his conditions for our relationship is that we tell the truth about everything and that we don't keep secrets. I expected that when he found out about my deceit, he would end the relationship, but his love for me is so strong that despite his heartbreak and anguish, he wanted to support me to get back to good health again. Since I revealed my secret, we have ended up having the best period of our entire relationship. Lachlan tried to help me stop, but I could not do it without professional help.

The cycle of trying to self-medicate my depression — taking drugs to lift myself up when I was down and then crashing even worse and needing to take more — had gone on for so long that I'd forgotten why I was using them in the first place. The drugs themselves had become the problem.

It was when I realised I was just as depressed on the drugs as I was off them that I decided to seek professional help. I realised that I didn't have all the answers. That there were other people who knew better than I did. That I couldn't do it by myself.

I brought matters to a head by confessing to my manager, Robyn Watson. I gave her the terrible news in September 2011. Telling Robyn would end my double life. I would have to choose between drugs and diving. Robyn, who loved and cared about me, was concerned and sympathetic. Her ultimatum for continuing to work with me was that I went into rehab and quit for good. Once she understood how serious I was about getting clean and getting to the Olympics, she gave me her support and said she would help me fight my addiction. I put together a strategy of how I was going to get and stay clean and prove it: I would go to rehab, attend Narcotics Anonymous (NA) meetings regularly and submit to continual drug testing so that there could be no day unaccounted for when I could've possibly used drugs.

In late September and October 2011, I entered a rehab hospital at Curl Curl, on Sydney's northern beaches, for three weeks of therapy, during which I would also attend NA meetings. The hospital treats people with addictions, anxiety, depression or eating disorders. I was one of about 30 inpatients in total, and I shared a room with five others. They made the place feel as homey as possible, with pictures on the walls and curtains around our beds so that we could have some personal space, each with our own furniture. There was a rec room, but we were discouraged from spending too much time in there, as the reason that most of us had addictions was because we had a knack for escaping our feelings by immersing ourselves in distracting activities. But we did have a chance twice a day, in the morning and in the afternoon, to take a walk on the beach, which was very therapeutic.

The idea of going into rehab was to address the issues that were making me a wounded adult–child and help me become a functional adult who could deal with the challenges of life without using drugs as a crutch. The focus was on finding out why I used and formulating an action plan for stopping for good. I came to know that there was a void in my life I was trying to fill with drugs. There was also shame at my hypocritically using drugs while pretending to be a good role model – yet my sorrow at being a sham could only be assuaged, I believed, *by* drugs. What a vicious cycle. What a mess. I had intensive therapy sessions to try to not rationalise my addictions but accept and then banish them.

On sheets of butcher's paper, we patients drew trauma eggs, large oval shapes, and wrote inside the eggs the times when we'd been traumatised – that is, suffered anything less than nurturing behaviour, ranging from being ignored to being abused. My egg was full. As I was drawing it, I was really dissociated from it – I thought I'd processed the traumatic events of my life already. But when I saw my egg up on the board in front of the group, I felt ashamed, and the walls came tumbling down, along with the tears.

I learnt that most of my trauma happened at 14, that the phrase 'I just want to be special' was my subconscious childhood motto, and that now all my self-worth had been riding on a gold medal in London, which was really unhealthy. We spoke about those traumatic occasions in the past, which had made me the person I was. I accepted that I had become a human doing, rather than a human being, always trying to achieve big things to win praise and affection. I had started out being good to stay in Mum's favour, and my thinking had escalated to the point where I believed that if I became the best in the world at something, as I did by winning a gold medal in Beijing in 2008, surely I would be the most loved and admired person on the planet. Of course, I realised in rehab, that didn't exactly follow. I began to understand that people loved me for who I was. Not what I achieved.

At rehab, we talked about being honest with yourself, love and hate, rage, too-high and too-low self-esteem, boundaries, the need for moderation, reality, vulnerability, rebelliousness, and the role of all of these in addiction, whether to drugs, alcohol, sex or gambling. We aired the subject of childhood trauma and the adult issues it can spawn. Children are egocentric, so they believe that anything that happens to them is their fault. A trauma, in this sense, is anything that causes a child to feel something bad about himself or herself. Even something as seemingly trivial as a parent not listening while the child reads can make that child feel worthless. The sense of worthlessness can resurface through life.

Also I came to realise in these sessions that I had a propensity to avoid my own feelings by taking care of others, trying to make them feel better so I feel better too. I raise my own self-esteem by raising others'.

Robyn came to see me in the visiting hour. In Family Week, the loved ones of patients were invited to sessions to improve communication. Lachlan came and – with brutal honesty, straight from the heart and without anger or blame – told me to my face what he felt about me and the damage my addiction was causing to me as a man, to him and to my diving career. I found myself thriving in the Family Week sessions. It was as if blinkers had been removed from my eyes. Having been emotionally numb for some time, the dam of all my constrained emotions suddenly burst.

Not only could I suddenly and clearly see solutions to my own problems, but at group sessions I was surprisingly able to offer insights into some of the other patients' emotional conundrums. A patient's wife broke out in a rash on her face, neck and chest and developed a funny taste in her mouth when her husband was discussing the reasons why he required rehab. It was clear to me that she was having a physical reaction to an emotional situation.

A woman in her mid-20s was in rehab because she had suffered from an eating disorder for a decade. Her mother was at the session. The girl admitted that she had not cried since she was 15. When she told her story, she did so without emotion and, in a flat monotone, she accused her mother of contributing to her condition. Her angry words were at odds with her dispassionate delivery. When it was her mother's turn to speak, she did not react to her daughter's accusations and seemed guarded in all she said. Here were two people discussing traumatic events as if they were recounting a trip to the park. It seemed clear that each was repressed, and I did know that suppression of one's feelings is a trait common to many addictions and eating disorders. The way I saw it — and the counsellor backed this up during the session — was that the mother had erected walls that were keeping her daughter out, and the daughter's angst at this had manifested itself in repression and an eating disorder.

One of the counsellors took me aside one day and said, 'Have you ever thought about taking up counselling as a career, Matthew? Because I think you would do really well'. I said that I might think about it one day, because I've always wanted to do a job where I can help people, but I needed to help myself before I helped anybody else.

My dad and Yollie and the kids came to visit me, too. That wasn't supposed to happen, because I hadn't told them of my addictions. Some weeks before I went into rehab, I had arranged for them to come to see me in Sydney. Then I entered the hospital and forgot all about it. Two days after the date on which we were meant to get together, I woke up in my bed in a cold sweat, suddenly remembering and feeling terrible that I had stood up people who had travelled so far to see me. I ran to the nurses' station and explained the situation and pleaded with the nurse to give me my mobile phone. I called my dad, who had been sick with worry that something had happened to me when I failed to show up and didn't answer my phone. I told him how sorry I was and that I was in hospital suffering from anxiety and depression.

They all came to visit me. Understandably, my dad wanted to know if him not being there for me as a child had contributed to my depression – and I had to tell him that I didn't know, because I didn't. I desperately wanted to tell him the real reason I was at the hospital, but I thought it was inappropriate to do so with the kids around, so I made the decision to wait until I got home before I called and told him the whole story. When I did, he was so supportive and understanding. He asked, 'Is there anything I can do? Is there anything Yolande and I can do?' He assured me that if there was anything I needed, I should let him know, because they were happy to help in any way. 'We just want to be any support that we can be for you,' he said.

One day towards the end of rehab, I suddenly had this thought: 'I can't ever have drugs again'. And then *boom*, I had a massive panic attack. I took it as a good sign: the addict inside, realising it had lost control, had issued a counter-attack.

On the day I left the hospital, I looked back at the massive changes I had made in the past few weeks. I had accepted I was a drug addict. I had gone to rehab. I had shopped around for a rehab centre that wasn't religious because I was really opposed to the idea of faith, and I had ended up not only opening up to it but begging a Higher Power to help me stay clean. I had spent my life escaping my feelings and now I had realised that I had to deal with my life and my feelings. And I had got past that 'wanting to want to quit' stage, and actually *wanted* to now.

When I was an addict, all the joy had been sucked out of my life. Diving had become an automated physical repetition. All my mental capacity for appreciating it or loving it had been taken away by addiction. Addiction reprograms your brain so that rather than finding joy in everyday tasks, you attribute any joy in life to whatever you're addicted to, in order to perpetuate the addiction.

While I was using drugs, I had completely lost any ability to reframe negative thoughts. A couple of months after rehab, I had a really nice sink-in moment one day at training. I was standing on the springboard and found myself thinking about how much I still had to do to get ready for the Olympics, and how little time I had left. It was all too much for me, and I thought, 'I can't do it'. Then, for the first time since using drugs, I actually changed my thought around and said, 'Yes, I can do it'. And I believed it. I had control of my thoughts again.

Rehab helped my diving in more ways than getting me off drugs. I became gentler with myself. I stopped thinking that anything other than gold in London would be a failure and that if I didn't win people would shun me. This made me happy, and if I was happy I dived well. I once felt that if I left no great Olympic legacy I would be totally forgotten. I knew after rehab that it was more important to be remembered for being a good person than as a gold medallist.

I still attend Narcotics Anonymous meetings, and I've done some serious soul searching. In April 2012, I was sitting in my car trying to locate my feelings and analyse them, and I began to cry as I realised with great clarity that my low self-esteem was a defence mechanism. I could never accept praise, because I believed that if you build yourself up you will inevitably fall. So when things were going well for me, I told myself bad things about myself, to bring myself down before outside forces did. It's my protection mechanism so I'm not caught off guard.

Many former addicts become addicted to other things: gambling, work, crossword puzzles, sugar. My one sin became the latter. I had this recurring thought that sugar would make me feel better. I used it to medicate my feelings and reward myself for doing well. I devoured Nutella and banana bread. I pulled into McDonald's restaurants for my regular fix of a small sundae with caramel on the bottom and chocolate on top, or sometimes the other way around. As I write, my sugar cravings are not as intense. Since I understood why I had these cravings I've been able to say no to them. I'm trying to be responsible in every aspect of my life, including diet. Besides, in the lead-up to London, Chava wanted me to lose a couple of kilos!

You see a lot of discouraging relapse statistics for the type of addiction I had, but I truly believe those statistics are unfounded. How could anybody actually know without following each and every former meth addict around once they leave rehab? And then there is the shame factor: once people have kicked the habit, they tend not to want to get involved with studies or anything that would reassociate them with that lifestyle, so I just don't know if we will ever be capable of getting fair, accurate statistics. And regardless, statistics can only paint a broad sense of the possible outcomes, while every individual is unique and has their own recovery path. I do believe that it is possible to change for the rest of your life, to no longer be an addict.

Mum has been so important in helping me to reclaim my life. She stepped up to the plate wonderfully, and even stopped drinking, in solidarity. She goes to AA meetings – we even go to addiction meetings together sometimes – and she is a changed woman. Me getting clean has helped her to get and stay sober, she says. Now she loves *not* drinking. She has more than atoned for some of the crazy things she did when I was a child. I know she feels uncomfortable about some aspects of our shared history, and I suggested that she consider doing a therapy session with me. She is still thinking it over. I'm sure that it would benefit us both. Lachlan may get involved, too, at some stage and the sessions may strengthen their relationship. Having said that, Lachlan and Mum are getting on really well.

Mum has lived in Sydney since March 2009, working first as a barista at the Manning Bar, at Sydney University. (She's mostly worked in hospitality, and I often joke that when the high school guidance counsellor asked her what she wanted to be, she must have put the emph-*a*-sis on the wrong sy-*lla*-ble, and that's how she ended up making coffee, not working as a lawyer.) Now she works as a housekeeper at a youth hostel in Glebe, in Sydney's inner west. Her depression started getting a bit better about six months to a year after she moved to Sydney, as she liked being closer to me. And things started improving exponentially for her once she stopped drinking.

Mum still hangs out with me, but it is so different to our old clubbing days in Brisbane, when everybody watched Mum and me throw emotional daggers at each other. We do healthy, wholesome things. Lachlan will cook a vegetarian meal for Mum, and then we'll play Kinect Bowling or Kinect Volleyball on the Xbox. And we actually have way more fun now.

To support my rehab and regular NA meetings, I also had hypnotherapy, which I believe helped. While under hypnosis, I was susceptible to messages that I do not need drugs or alcohol.

I have been seeing a psychologist weekly in an effort to learn to value myself not just as a diver but as a person.

I had depended too much on diving for reinforcement of my self-worth and to win affection from friends and the public. When my stress fractures and ab injury prevented me from diving, I no longer had that source of adulation and positive reinforcement. I had to realise that I am a good, kind and decent person with a number of positive personality traits and valuable skills, who just happens to be an awesome diver.

I now understand that I was using drugs to compensate for a void in my life, yet I still can't put my finger on exactly what that void is. I would seem to have it all. I am in love and am loved. I have staunch friends. I won an Olympic gold medal and was at the top of my sport for some years. I have mended my fences with my mum and come to know my dad. My future post-diving looks bright. Maybe one day I'll unearth the root of my former addiction, whether it derived from my past, my family, diving traumas, my sexuality, the pressures of success – maybe the cause was a combination of all of these. As I write these words, I am still in therapy, doing my best to become a healthier, happier person. I'm just scratching the surface. The answers continue to elude me. I may work it out one day.

15

london bound

As I made my run to qualify for the London Olympics, to be held in July–August 2012, the rivalry intensified between Tom Daley, British diving's boy wonder, and me. We were both considered to be fine divers and free spirits with strong fan followings. Tom beat me in some important competitions in 2010, and my ab tear then prevented me from competing in FINA events the following year and re-establishing my reputation as the world's top 10 metre platform diver.

All through 2011, Tom was feted by the media and public as a probable gold medal winner at the London Games. To read a lot of what was written and said about him, all he had to do was turn up on the 10 metre platform at the Games and the gold medal was as good as around his neck. I didn't stand a chance, and nor did the Chinese diver Qiu Bo. Admittedly, it was not Tom saying this, but the media. Nevertheless, I was jealous at the fuss that was being made of Daley. Building Tom up so shamelessly was putting tremendous pressure on him – and, frankly, as his competitor, it was pressure that I was happy for him to bear.

As London approached, the word was that Tom's coaches were worried that expectations placed on him to win gold at his hometown Games were too high and were undermining his preparation, as were the number of celebrity events that he was attending, and the extracurricular – and, in my opinion, counterproductive – invitations he was saying yes to. He even made a video of himself and the British diving team dancing on a beach to LMFAO's 'Sexy and I Know It', which was a YouTube sensation.

Tom, I reasoned, was a nice boy at heart, and in the early days of our rivalry we got on very well. But it now *was* personal between Tom and me. Our rivalry was not a media invention. At the Commonwealth Games in Delhi, Tom scored seven perfect 10s from the judges with his third dive, an inward three and a half somersault. The dive was instrumental in him winning the final. It was also the very same dive for which I had gained a perfect score in the World Cup in China that June. I did believe that I could beat Tom. I respected him greatly as a rival – yet, while saying that, I put him, and all the other divers, out of my mind. I was content to embrace the role of the underdog that had been assigned to me by the press. What I was about was, first, making it to London, and then doing the best dives I could.

In December 2011, as I flew to Adelaide to compete in the Australian National Open Championships at the South Australian Aquatic & Leisure Centre at Marion, I knew what I had to do between then and the Olympics. I had to get back into my Beijing mindset that Chava had devised for me: relax; enjoy the experience; dive the best dive I can; be happy up there on the platform, because if people are wanting me to win I can sense that and it somehow improves my performance.

I began chanting the Serenity Prayer in my head before a dive as a relaxation tool. I had learned it in rehab, and they say it at the end of every Narcotics Anonymous meeting. The prayer eased the pressure too: 'God, give me the serenity to accept the things I cannot change; courage to change the things I can; and wisdom to know the difference'. What this meant to me in a diving context is that it would be the London Olympics judges' job, not mine, to compare the divers' performances and decide who had done the best. There was no point in worrying about my rivals, just the things I could control. I couldn't control how Tom Daley or Qiu Bo would dive, whether they dived superbly or muffed it. I *could* control my own practice, my own choice of dive, my own fitness, my own relaxed frame of mind, my own performance.

Kenneth Graham, the NSWIS physiologist, was an integral part of my preparation. He is a wizard on such things as when and how to sleep to perform at your peak, techniques to overcome jet lag (he supplied us with noise-cancelling headphones to eliminate plane engine noise and also masks to keep the air we breathed in planes moist) and get acclimatised and into synch with time zones when we compete overseas. He reads all the latest medical studies and systematises everything mathematically. When I was training for the Beijing Olympics, he did a projection of my likely scores and those of my competitors and, by and large, he was spot-on. He did the same for me for 2009 and 2010. For the London Olympics, he worked out what score I would need to win a medal and, taking degree of difficulty into account, counselled Chava and me on which dives I would need to perform well to attain that score.

At the Nationals in Adelaide, I proved that I was on course for the Olympics. Obviously because I had not dived for so long, I was nervous, yet they were healthy, not toxic, nerves. I won the final, despite still being in some pain from my abdominal tear and diving a reduced list to protect my ab. My dives were: front three and a half pike, back three and a half tuck, reverse two and a half tuck (modified from my usual three and a half tuck to protect my ab), arm-stand back double two and a half twist, an inward three and a half, and a back two and a half somersault two and a half twist. I got these dives together just before the Nationals, because I could not dive until weeks before. I was back as the best 10 metre platform diver in Australia – but far more important, I felt good, and instead of being overwhelmed by fears and desperation, I was filled with confidence about the coming Olympic year.

I didn't have a problem with Diving Australia any more. We had all changed our attitude. What mattered was not interstate politics but that Australia did well. As Chava's team was accumulating medals and word had spread that he ran a happy set-up, other Queensland divers were leaving Brisbane for Sydney. Hui had warmed to me – he was friendly to me when our paths crossed. And, having gone through all that I had, in sport and personally, I was a lot more mature now. Though I had my moments, I was much less of a brat. I was again, in theory and reality, a good ambassador and role model and spokesperson for diving.

Best of all, I had stopped being tormented by worry that I was a fraud. I was happy in my skin and noticing clouds and butterflies, when before I was so conflicted I'd look right past them. At last I was able to admire beauty and let it seep into my senses. I could represent my sponsors and speak to kids about being the best that they could be and how they must strive to make their dreams come true, without shuddering with shame that I was only talking the talk, not walking the walk. Yes, I had run off the rails, but now I was back on track for life and for London.

16

olympic fever

My 2012 Olympic campaign began in earnest in early February when I flew to Rostock, Germany, for the year's first FINA Grand Prix event. My schedule of events was Rostock, then the World Cup in London, the Australian Olympic trials in Adelaide, FINA Grand Prix events in Montreal and Fort Lauderdale, and then the Olympic Games in August, where, if I stayed healthy and in form, I would compete in the 10 metre platform event at the spanking new London Olympic Aquatic Centre diving pool. Chava's plan for me was to gradually hone my fitness and technique, get my ab right and be at my peak for the Games.

To counter the high expectations that were being placed on me and the feelings I still occasionally had that I would be thought a failure if I didn't win everything in this Olympic year, including an Olympic gold medal, Chava repeated endlessly, 'You're a great diver. If you dive at your best, then that will be enough to win'. He said to use the Rostock Grand Prix and the World Cup events to test the waters. He reminded me that I only placed fifth at the World Cup before the Olympics in 2008 … which was immaterial when I dived at the Games.

Before I left Australia, my manager, Robyn Watson, asked me what my goals were for the London Olympics. I told her that I wanted simply to do my best. She said, 'Good answer. For some of my other athletes, the major goal is just to qualify, and they'll be happy with that no matter if they come last in London. Others on my books are so determined to win a gold medal and so obsessing over the other competitors that they'll be super-stressed and throwing up at poolside'.

In Rostock, I had some problems with the thicker platform they use there — it's 40 centimetres thick, whereas the Australian platform is just 16 centimetres. Twice during training I hit the platform with my feet mid-dive, one time so hard that I lost my rotation and hit the water flat on my back first and surfaced coughing up blood. Because the blood vessels in the lungs are so fine, the impact had pushed the blood out of them into the air sacs of my lungs. There was a welt across my entire back, and in between my shoulder blades there was a circle the size of a wedding ring in which the force had pushed whiteheads deep into my pores and pimples had sprung up. The ankle that had knocked the platform was sore for a couple of weeks.

That accident freaked me out. Normally when you dive from a handstand position facing the water, you use your arms to launch yourself *up* off the platform, while you flick your legs *out*, away from the platform. But with my hurt abdominal muscle, I didn't have as much power in my upper body as before, so I was pushing *out* with my arms and flicking my legs *down*, underneath the platform, to get myself the rotation that I needed to do a somersault. My flick clipped the underside of the 40cm platform, whereas with my usual 16cm platform I would have more space to come underneath and so my feet wouldn't touch. I modified my technique and was back on the platform for the prelims two days later. In the finals, I came fifth, and the place-getters were Chen Aisen and Xie Siyi of China and Germany's Martin Wolfram. I was satisfied with that performance given the difficulties I'd had because of the thickness of the platform.

'Stinking thinking' is the term I use for the dangerous and counterproductive ruminations I have had in the past. It was creeping up on me again. At night, I was having nightmares about hitting the platform. I was constantly being jolted awake by this sickening sensation of freefalling through the air.

I had cut down on my visits to a psychologist since the end of 2011, and I felt I needed some help to prevent the stinking thinking taking hold. So when I arrived in London from Rostock, I saw sports psychologist Ruth Anderson, the head of the psychology section of the Olympic Medical Centre in London. I hadn't used a sports psychologist since my years in Brisbane when I sought help to manage my interactions with Hui Tong because our problems were affecting my diving. Since I had been with Chava I had no such strife in my diving life. I saw Ruth Anderson because I feared that if my stinking thinking recurred it would harm my diving form in this important Olympic year. Ruth, who before becoming a sports psychologist had worked with people suffering drug-induced psychoses, was terrific.

She taught me to use cognitive behavioural therapy and visualisation to reframe and keep my bad thoughts at bay. She could tell I lacked self-confidence, and she gave me ways to acknowledge my achievements and not let myself be engulfed by negativity. She suggested that each night before I went to bed I watch videos of training sessions in London in which I had dived well. Now when I closed my eyes, the image I had in my mind was of one of my successful dives, and I began to sleep peacefully again.

When I arrived in London for the World Cup, it had been 18 months since I had competed truly injury free. I was back to international competition standard, but not quite back to where I was when I won the event in 2010. My ab had recovered, but because I'd been forced to take a break from diving while it healed, I had lost a lot of strength and was still trying to get it back. I was about halfway to where I needed to be at the Olympics, not yet having worked up to my back three and a half somersault pike. I was still able to replicate my Beijing-winning dive in practice, and when I did, there was spontaneous applause from the coaches, other athletes and the few media who were poolside at the London Olympic Aquatic Centre.

In London at the Olympic diving pool, the platform is 31cm thick, not as thick as at Rostock, but still much thicker than Australian platforms, and my problems continued. In the prelims I was awarded 8.5s for my arm-stand dive. This was higher than my and Chava's expectations. But then in the semi-final, compensating for my lack of upper body strength again, I scraped the underside of the platform once more and knocked myself off-balance, cartwheeling out of the dive and hitting the water anything but gracefully. For that I was awarded miserable 4s and 4.5s and did not make the finals. Qiu Bo won the event, beating the second place-getter Victor Minibaev by 50 points. Obviously, he was going to be the one to beat at the Olympics. With 414.70 points, I came thirteenth, missing the finals by just one place. True to our philosophy, I was unfazed. As world champion, Qiu Bo was entitled to Olympic favouritism; yet Zhou Luxin was everyone's pick to win gold at Beijing, and the pressure got the better of him.

My semi-final dive was a disaster, but an aberration that I could easily fix, and I was really happy with my prelim dives considering that before the World Cup I had only been diving for six weeks injury free. If not for the botched dive in the semi, I would have breezed into the finals. The dives I had completed successfully boosted my confidence and made me appreciate anew what I was capable of in elite competition.

I had become familiar with the London Olympic diving venue when I'd visited it in August 2011 to film some Olympic promos while I was on holidays. As always, I'd had my ukulele with me, and I played 'Cherry' by Amy Winehouse. I've always had a special place in my heart for her, and that is one of my favourite songs to play. It was awesome: playing Amy Winehouse, a British icon, in an iconic London venue before it had even opened.

But that hadn't been enough to make me completely comfortable with the diving pool at the London Aquatic Centre. Apart from the 31cm thickness of the 10 metre platform, the ceiling above it is stark, dark grey and dips in a wave formation. There are clusters of lights in it. With its waves, the ceiling made me feel claustrophobic. It seemed very close when I was standing on the platform, almost as if

Underwater funsies at London 2012

That 'controversial' picture from the London Games. Did I get in trouble? Well, the police were watching the whole time, and the Australian chef de mission Nick Green was so impressed he asked me to email the picture to him. So, umm… no.

Welcome to London 2012, with my coach Chava Sobrino and training partner Melissa Wu.

The lining of our Opening Ceremony jackets had the name of every Australian Olympic gold medallist throughout history.

The big reveal: showing off the Opening Ceremony outfit to the media at a press conference, with equally dapper team mates Brittany Broben and Loudy Wiggins.

The Australian Olympic Diving Team for London 2012.

The entire Aussie Olympic team got to walk all over me… and every other Australian gold medallist to date.

Me and two 'Volley-unteers' went through almost 50 pairs of Dunlops to find ones that had my name in the insole. I was so excited when I found them that I took the insoles out so I wouldn't wear out my name by marching in them.

Opening Ceremony night. While the divers didn't actually march, we still got dressed up and congregated with all the other Aussies to take photos and enjoy the atmosphere.

Me and 'Mitch's Bitches': Anabelle Smith, Jaele Patrick, Brittany Broben and Rachel Bugg.

The athletes that didn't go in the Opening Ceremony did a march of their own around the athletes' village. Ours was a little less structured though, with countries intermingling and some 'non-participants' coming along for the ride! (With US diver Cassidy Krug.)

The benefit of having disproportionately long limbs is the ability to take a self-portrait of so many good-looking people in one shot: the Aussie diving contingent, minus the oldies.

For the Australian Olympic Team reception, Melissa Wu and I were asked to model the appropriate attire for flyers to be put up throughout the Aussies' building. I think they picked us because we were dubbed 'the wonderful Twitters of Oz' by the media for our prolific tweeting of pictures of ourselves. Clearly not camera shy.

Team mate Anabelle Smith and I with probably my favourite person on the team, Australian basketballer Liz Cambage. No, she's not wearing heels. Yes, she is nice to cuddle.

Hanging out in the grandstand watching the competition with team mate Anabelle Smith, my coach Chava, and the team's head psychologist Ruth Anderson.

View of the Olympic Stadium at night (from the Westfield in London Olympic Park). I actually took this picture when I did a whole bunch of media after the men's 10m platform final.

This is my favourite picture of my training partner, Melissa Wu – luckily, it's also a nice picture of my coach Chava and me, too.

This page is pretty much just pictures of me climbing on stuff in the athletes' village.

At the Aussies' recovery centre – set up in a school for severely disabled children during their summer holidays. Perfect for contrast (hot and cold) therapy and ice baths … the ball pit was just a fun bonus!

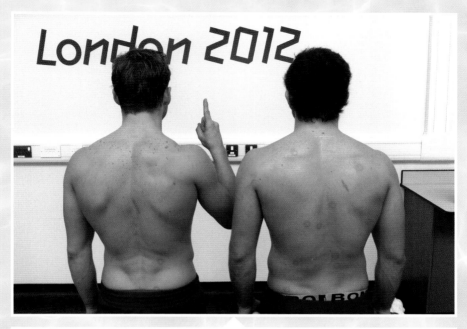

And different kinds of recovery: sting pong (the victor gets to belt a ball at the loser's back from the other end of the table… clearly, I was the victor). With Ethan Warren, my 3m and 10m synchro partner from Delhi 2010.

Food recovery… 'I'm Australian, don't judge me.'

Laughter therapy, with Hamish and Andy.

Making amends: my former coach, Hui Tong and I getting on like a house on fire. Sometimes his is the only voice I can distinguish in the crowd before my dives. We also connected over our passion for playing table tennis.

Cheeky friends: Tom Daley trying to replicate my infamous 'rings picture' at the beginning of this photo section. I laughed. A lot.

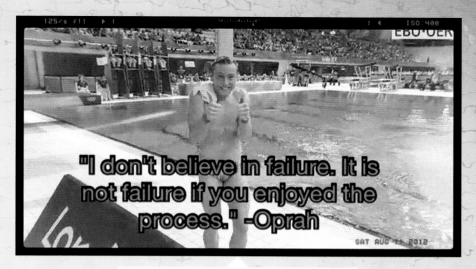

"I don't believe in failure. It is not failure if you enjoyed the process." -Oprah

SAT AUG 11 2012

Amen sista! – one of my fans sent me this on Twitter, and it really resonated with me.

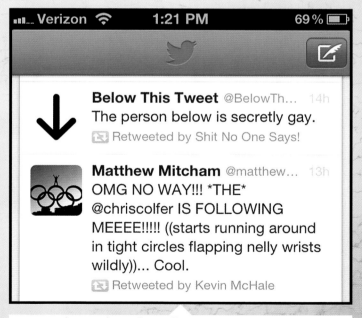

Below This Tweet @BelowTh... 14h
The person below is secretly gay.
🔁 Retweeted by Shit No One Says!

Matthew Mitcham @matthew... 13h
OMG NO WAY!!! *THE* @chriscolfer IS FOLLOWING MEEEE!!!!! ((starts running around in tight circles flapping nelly wrists wildly))... Cool.
🔁 Retweeted by Kevin McHale

Anyone who watches 'Glee' will appreciate this. This was my reaction when I realised Kurt (the gay character on Glee) was following me, which was retweeted by Artie (the character in a wheelchair) and the irony of the tweet above is priceless.

In Rome, recording a ukulele video (a mash-up of Morcheeba's 'Rome Wasn't Built In A Day' and B-52s' 'Roam') on my friend Jonathan's terrace, where we have spent several summers eating, talking and playing cards.

Showing off (my muscular legs) in Villa Borghese in Rome.

Lachlan and I doing a Segway tour of Rome. I paid the money just to ride around on it for three hours – but all the historical monuments we visited along the way were a nice bonus.

When I got home from the London Olympics, I found out I had been named one of the top 10 most influential under 30 year olds on social media – at the event with the host Tom Waterhouse and Prime Minister Julia Gillard.

I was in pretty good company, too… but I'm not going to name them all because I just don't have time for that.

'Photographing Matthew Mitcham #4' by William Yang,
part of the Matt Dive Gold exhibition.

'The Adventures of Droplet the Elf' by Majorcan artist Francesca Martí,
another image from the Matt Dive Gold exhibition.

Unconditional support from mentors and friends: diving legend Greg Louganis and Olympic diving judge Simon Latimer.

CCTV Chinese Television took me on the Sydney Harbour Bridge Climb to do an interview on Chinese New Year (2011) because according to the Chinese, it brings good luck to climb a peak on such an auspicious day.

Divers from Canada, Mexico, Brazil, Australia and the US come together in Fort Lauderdale in a display of international cooperation in motion. Well, we were actually there for the USA Grand Prix, but this was certainly the highlight of the competition.

Taken at the Watsons Bay harbour pool, this is probably my favourite image (of myself) of all time. It reminds me of the best summer of my life: living in our friend John's living room in Watsons Bay because we couldn't afford a place of our own. Along with the wonderful memories, I love the graceful lines of my dive and the juxtaposition of that dude going ass-over-tit in the background.

I could reach up and touch it. I prefer a light and bright pool. Usually in diving pools, the 5 metre platform is below the 10 metre, but in London it is way off to the side. I use the 5 metre platform as a point of reference to gauge how high I am in my dives, and in London you can't see it. In practice Chava had to call to me the right time to come out of my dive.

That World Cup was a recce expedition, getting used to the London pool and having a close look at my rivals. On their showings at the World Cup and in the past 12 months, it was obvious that Qiu Bo and the Russian Minibaev were in the running for Olympic medals. Both are brilliant divers. Qiu Bo is a machine and Minibaev can perform difficult, and therefore high scoring, dives well, yet he can be inconsistent. I believed that so long as I dived my best, I would have a chance, too, and that my fate was in my hands.

Of course, Tom Daley would be a contender for gold, although in the World Cup the only event he contested was the 10 metre synchro with his fellow Briton Peter Waterfield. The pair came seventh. In later Grand Prix events he would fare much better. Tom had been out of sorts. He was dealing with the loss of his father to brain cancer in May 2011. It also seemed his commitments were out of control, because he himself said that he was having trouble trying to handle the distractions and the enormous expectations of his nation to be at his best at the Olympics.

The media was still fixated on him. So much so that when I gave a 15 minute interview to a group of London journalists during the World Cup, they edited out everything I said about my own form and prospects and retained in their stories only a comment I made in response to the ones Tom had made about the burden of all the distractions and public expectations. I didn't realise how tabloid the British press is; they'll do anything for a sensational headline. Typical was: 'Mitcham Says Daley Can't Have His Cake and Eat It Too'.

When I read the article, I was mortified. My words made me sound superior and bitchy, like some old windbag giving unsought advice. I fronted Tom and told him that I was sorry for the way the interview had come out. He was understanding and told me not to worry about it.

For a change, the newspapers brought good tidings when I read that Australia's head coach, Hui Tong, rated me 'a high chance' of becoming the first back-to-back 10 metre platform gold medallist since Greg Louganis in 1988. Hui said, 'Matthew's raw ability and determination will ensure he will remain a force to be reckoned with'. I valued Hui's opinion, and his generous words meant so much to me. He had changed and I had changed. I could hear him cheering for me during the Rostock and London World Cup competitions, and at Rostock he was the only one in the Australian team who filmed my dives.

Back home, I trained my arse off for the next pre-Olympic event, the Diving Nomination Trials for the 2012 Australian Olympic Team in Adelaide in early April. I was feeling better than I had in some time. My ab was not hurting me, and I was buoyed by my performances in Germany and London. I was motivated and determined. I would work on perfecting my hardest dives, building up my strength and attaining consistency, and hopefully when the Australian team was named in late May I would be in it.

On March 2, I turned 24, and felt very, very old because of everything I'd experienced, physically and mentally.

As a birthday gift to myself, I went to Queensland to visit my father, Greg, and his family and my grandma. Apart from seeing them, I did have an ulterior motive. I wanted to be anywhere but in Sydney when the Gay and Lesbian Mardi Gras was on. That partying environment wasn't for me any more. When I returned to Sydney from Queensland and went to a post-Mardi Gras barbecue, I was glad I had made that choice. It seemed that all my friends were talking about were how great the drugs were. I felt strong and good about myself.

I was determined to continue feeling that way not just for the Olympics but for the rest of my life. I congratulated myself that I had come far since rehab. I had the odd bouts of stinking thinking, but I wasn't going to weaken. I had won at Beijing because my head and body were in the right place.

I trained hard and was focused and did not knock myself about, and as that regime worked for me in Beijing, I would now follow a similar plan. The London Games were just four months away.

At home, life with Lachlan had never been better. I loved and was loved in return. We had been through a lot, and come out of the hard times stronger and happier than ever. As Lachlan says, 'We are together, and we are our own people as well, and that's healthy. We're very happy'. Of course, being the partner of a diver has its challenges for Lachlan. I am so busy with training, travelling to compete, and obligations for my sponsors that we don't get much of a chance to curl up at night and watch our favourite TV shows together, like *Nurse Jackie*, *Raising Hope*, *Star Trek*. I don't have time to do much about the house, and Lachlan does most of the cooking. No doubt Lachlan will get his own back whenever I finally retire from diving.

Olympic excitement was mounting. As the London reporters had, Australian journalists wanted to talk to me, but they wanted to talk to me about *me* ... not Tom Daley. Mostly it was about my London prospects, although some wanted to know my views on the hot topic of the day, gay marriage. I told them that while I'm still too young for it to be on the agenda for me personally, I believe that anybody who wants to get married should be allowed to. Footage of my performance at Beijing started popping up on TV as part of London Games teasers on the Olympic networks.

At the Diving Nomination Trials, I made a statement. While I did OK in the preliminary and semi-finals, I dived very well indeed in the finals. In my fifth dive, a back three and a half tuck, I scored straight perfect 10s. I scored two 10s on my arm-stand back triple tuck, which I had only relearned the week before; two 10s on my inward three and a half tuck; 9s on my front three and a half pike; 8.5s on my reverse three and a half tuck; and 8.5s for my back two and a half somersault two and a half twist. That was good. I won the final, and I felt I could improve enough to score 570, the score that Chava and I believed would be necessary to win a medal in London, and which would be a new personal best for me. It was nice to be back. Everything I was doing was starting to work and fall into place. It was the first time since my ab injury that I had dived without even worrying about pain. I felt I was back on par with the best divers in the world.

I went straight back to hard training after the trials. My strength coach had me doing land-saults with weights attached to my ankles. I planned to perfect the back three and a half somersault pike and the arm-stand back twist that I would be reintroducing to my repertoire in the upcoming FINA Grand Prix events in Montreal and Fort Lauderdale. I had been substituting a back three and a half somersault tuck instead of the more taxing pike, and while I received 10s from all the judges for it, it has only a 3.2 degree of difficulty, whereas with the pike it is worth 3.6. I still did not know if my ab would stand up to the pike in the Olympics. I realised that I may have to make do with the tuck.

With just 100 days to go until the Olympic Games Opening Ceremony, I appeared at a press conference with other athletes. I told the gathering how excited I was and that I hoped to do well. Someone asked me if I was feeling the pressure. I replied, 'It's a really hard position for me to be in to be the reigning Olympic champion because people are seeing me as going to London to defend my title, and I see that as a very hard position to be in because anything other than a win is going to seem like a failure. I'm trying to reframe it in my own mind just to take the pressure off and think that I've already won an Olympic gold medal so anything on top of this is a bonus. I've been doing a lot of psychology around it, because I was finding it was starting to get really overwhelming for me last year when I was out of the pool because of this injury. It was starting to get closer and closer to the Games, and I was worried whether or not I'd be ready for the Olympics and whether or not I should even bother. I have such high expectations and high standards, I thought there's no point me going to the Olympics unless I think I can win.'

I said that doing well at the Olympic trials and scoring all those perfect 10s meant that I was starting to get back to my old form, and the result had given me confidence. However, I continued, 'while the score that I got [at the trials] was better than my Olympic final score in 2008, I feel like there's a lot more improvement to go, which is really exciting for me because the standard of diving has improved a lot and I reckon I can top that again'.

Then, just days before flying out for the Montreal Grand Prix event, I strained my right ab, which had been compensating for the reduced functionality of my left abdominal muscle. I immediately had another Platelet Rich Plasma injection to try to repair the strain, and had a week of reduced training. I ruled myself out of the Montreal competition and buckled down to get fit in time to compete at Fort Lauderdale. I despaired. My old feelings of being a fraud resurfaced, because at the function to mark 100 days until the Games I had told the media that my ab was 100 percent recovered and I could now train at full volume to win a gold medal. I wanted sponsors to gain confidence in me again, not think I was injured and a wasted investment. I believed I had deceived everyone by being so cocky. I found myself in the unfortunate position of covering up my new injury. Diving Australia quietly scratched me from Montreal and rearranged my air travel straight to Fort Lauderdale, where I came seventh in the semi-finals, just missing out on a place in the finals.

I felt like a broken-down old hack. If I was a horse, I'd be shot and sent off to the glue factory.

But I wasn't giving up. The Olympics were what I'd been training for, and I was going to give it my best. That's the spirit of the Olympics. And I had to prove to myself that despite everything I had faced, I could do this.

17

all bets are off

I thought I would probably retire at the end of the London Games because platform diving wasn't going to become any less damaging and wearing on my body, and the accidents I'd had earlier in the year – hitting the platform with my foot and becoming disoriented mid-air – had begun to affect me.

Fearlessness had been a big advantage for me when I started out in diving, but the older I got, the wiser I became. Self-preservation had kicked in. I thought about the repercussions if I had a serious accident. Diving from a height of 10 metres, a moment's misjudgment could seriously maim, paralyse or kill me.

Now I was scared every time I went up to the platform, even if I was doing a dive in which I'd never had an accident before. I was continually second guessing myself. Just before my take-off, I would think, 'Am I going to hurt myself?'

Before the team left Australia, I chatted about retirement with 20-year-old Melissa Wu, who won silver in the women's 10 metre platform in Beijing. We told each other that London was the end of the line for us.

So one morning I got a bit of a surprise when I heard Chava and Melissa discussing how much time she was going to have off after London before she got back into training.

And then Chava turned to me and said, 'How much time are you having off?'

I supposed that I could always take a couple of years off, get refreshed and then see if I wanted to come back to the sport. 'I don't know,' I said. 'I was thinking a couple of years.'

'Oh, I was thinking a couple of weeks,' he replied. It was classic Chava. Months earlier, he had expressed how keen he was for Melissa and Alex and me to go to the Glasgow Commonwealth Games with him. Knowing that I was considering giving up diving, he now offered up Plan B: I could switch to the 3 metre springboard after London. I would need to build up more strength in my legs, but overall springboard diving is less damaging on the body. And the accident risk is reduced, because if you wipe out it's not like you're going to bleed into the lungs, or worse. Chava and I began having a casual, ongoing conversation about the idea, but as I headed to London I was still leaning towards retiring altogether.

Once I got there, though, all bets were off. Suddenly I remembered what an amazing experience it is to be in the Olympic village. People from all over the world come together to form a community in which gender, nationality and sporting differences are irrelevant. There is no animosity, acrimony or tension between people of different nations, and everyone shows the utmost respect to everyone else. There is a universal feeling of solidarity and camaraderie that you don't see anywhere else in the world. I called the village a utopian prison, because with a high fence topped with barbed wire, armed guards and security screening points, it had characteristics of a minimum-security jail – just one that was filled with beautiful, fit people who all got along with one another!

I later told a journalist that my plans for retirement had gone out the window, because being at the Olympics was the best, most addictive experience. (There was a hidden meaning in my use of the word 'addictive', an extra significance for me that other people weren't aware of.) I never want to miss another Olympics again, whether I am there as a competitor, a commentator or a spectator.

I arrived six days before the Opening Ceremony, giving me almost three weeks to get used to diving in the aquatic centre. We had a training session each morning and afternoon, but we had the middle of the day to ourselves.

Soon after we arrived, I did a lap of the village with a few other Australian athletes.

After we'd scoped the place out, we set off on a photographic expedition. Of course everyone wanted their photo taken with the Olympic rings. Athletes from every nation had been posing for pictures under them. But I thought we should go one better, so I gave James Connor, the 17-year-old diver from Brisbane, a boost to one of the bottom rings, where he had his picture taken. We swapped places so I could have my photo taken there, too.

And then I had the bright idea of shimmying to the top of the rings and standing up there. It was late in the afternoon, and by the time I'd made it to the top, the sun had set behind the buildings. You couldn't see the poles supporting the rings — just the rings kind of hovering in mid-air, with my little silhouette on top and the beautiful dusk skyline behind. It all came together perfectly. I put the picture up on Twitter, and the vast majority of the public's and the media's reaction was really positive.

But when I posted a couple of other pics I took for fun — me planking on the head of a gorilla statue and doing a one-armed handstand on a turtle sculpture — some of the Australian media started putting a different spin on it, saying that the way I had posed on the rings was risky and dangerous and unwise. That was pretty funny because I do handstands on the edge of a platform that's 10 metres high and the Olympic rings are only about six metres off the ground. It's just the angle of the photo that makes them look much taller than they actually are.

Along with my teammates Brittany Broben and Loudy Wiggins, the next day I did a press conference to show off the new Australian uniforms, and one of the journalists there asked whether I got in trouble for climbing the Olympic rings. But I hadn't broken any rules. There were police patrolling the village all the time, keeping an eye on things, and a couple of cops had been standing there, totally unfazed, watching me climb up. At the press conference, I was sitting next to Nick Green, the Australian chef de mission, and he actually told me he thought the photo was awesome and asked me to email it to him, so I wasn't exactly worried about getting in trouble from officialdom, either.

I met Dawn Fraser in the village the next day. The stir I'd caused was nothing compared to what happened to her after the 1964 Tokyo Games, when she helped someone climb a flagpole to pinch an Olympic flag as a souvenir. That had ended her career, because though she wasn't charged and the police actually gave her the flag, the Australian swimming governing body suspended her and she couldn't train for the next Games. Dawn and I bonded over the fact that we are from the same 'hood, Balmain, and I took a photo of her with her grandson. She was wonderful and had some words of wisdom for me: 'You know how to do it; you've done it before. Just go and do your job and don't worry about what anybody else says'.

Another thing I did between training sessions was to unleash my ukulele playing and singing on YouTube after someone on Twitter asked me to. I was very self-conscious when I shot the first video, Beyoncé's 'Single Ladies', which I did in my room at the athletes' village. Because I felt trepidation about sharing it with the world, I backlit it so you could hardly tell it was me. But I got a really positive response when I posted it. There were only a handful of dislikes and a lot of likes, which gave me the courage to do another one. People had made comments about the lighting in the first one. They thought I was just bad at lighting, not that I was hiding in the shadows on purpose. So I lit myself properly for the next one, a rendition of the theme song from my favourite TV show, *Family Guy*. I did it in my room, too, but now you could see the posters and letters and cards that I'd stuck on my wall.

Having a Twitter community to share the Olympic experience with was awesome, and I couldn't believe it when my idol Stephen Fry actually started following me. I tried to play it cool, but it was the biggest fan girl moment of my life. Stephen Fry is an artist with the English language. He's witty and smart, really humble and successful across all platforms, whether he's on the stage or on TV or writing books. Everything he does, he just does it really well. And I love that he hasn't done anything with his nose; it's so distinctive.

I found out that a few other famous people were also following me on Twitter – Chris Colfer and Kevin McHale, who play Kurt and Artie on *Glee*, and Jake Shears from The Scissor Sisters. These guys, and Stephen Fry, have got millions of followers, so having them following me just blew my mind. After the Olympics I found out there was a study showing that while I didn't have the most Twitter followers compared with other members of the Australian team, I was the most influential based on levels of influence, popularity, engagement and trust. The reason I'm such a prolific tweeter is that I want people to be able to share in the things I'm experiencing. My #bitchams, #mitchamigos, #mattadores and everyone who sent me tweets were incredibly supportive the whole time I was away, and it meant a lot to me.

Before the competition began, I wanted to clear my conscience regarding things I'd said to journalists in the past about Tom Daley. I felt genuine regret about being critical of Tom for the comments he had made about the pressure he was feeling from the media and the public to win at these Olympics. My comments had stemmed from jealousy that

Tom was getting so much media attention. So before I left for London, I sent him a Facebook message apologising. I wanted to be able to compete with clean karma.

My other reason for sending him a message was that I genuinely wanted to be friends with him. He is a nice kid with a good head on his shoulders, and by making those comments in the media I had jeopardised what could potentially be a good friendship. I hoped that putting my contrite feelings out there and showing my vulnerability would yield a positive effect on our relationship – and it really did. Tom and I ended up being good friends in London. My little sister, Mia, thinks Tom is just sex on legs. The Brits had made up Tom Daley masks, so in return for a couple of packets of Tim Tams I'd brought from Sydney, I got him to sign the back of one with the words, 'Your brother is awesome, Love Tom'.

In London I had the chance to strengthen my relationship with another person who's important to me, Hui Tong, my former coach from Brisbane. When the Australian divers discovered that the gym at the Olympic village had a few ping pong tables, everyone wanted to have a go, but Hui and I were the ones who were the most excited about it. While we were playing together, I just had this big smile on my face, thinking about what a contrast this was to the past. It was a beautiful example of how much our relationship had changed. I wish I had a picture of us playing ping pong, but at least I got one of us sitting side by side in the dining hall, arms slung around each other's shoulders. I am profoundly grateful to Hui for everything he has done for me, and I'm thankful that our relationship has come such a long way and is now filled with mutual respect.

The whole time during training in London I wasn't diving to my usual standard. My body wasn't as strong as it should have been. I felt slow and sluggish, and my dives lacked refinement. Because of the injuries I'd had, I simply needed more time to prepare. I trained hard, trying to make myself as ready as possible, but my ab was still playing up and I had to have a couple of needles in it while I was there.

When I do an inward three and a half somersault, I spot the lights in the ceiling to orientate myself. In the London venue, the lights are clustered randomly rather than being in uniform rows on the ceiling, which made it hard for me to use them to spot. The first time I did an inward three and a half during training, I thought I had done an extra half a somersault than I had, so I became disoriented and had a mini freak out. Fortunately I entered the water the right way round, because Chava called when I needed to come out of the dive. From that point onwards, I compensated for the different position of the lights by holding on for a bit longer before coming out of my dive so that I completed the full three and a half somersaults. For more than a week I still asked Chava to call me out of my dives.

I decided that at the Olympics I would not do the arm-stand back two and a half twist that had caused me problems at the World Cup in London in 2011, when my foot scraped the underside of the platform and I cartwheeled out of my dive. I was too scared to use that dive again and would substitute an arm-stand back triple somersault.

At least the challenge I'd had at the World Cup of not being able to gauge how far I was from the water during my back three and a half somersault wasn't an issue any more. They had stuck a big white London 2012 logo about halfway up the 10 metre tower, and I was able to use that as a guide.

In the preliminary round, 32 divers would compete and the 18 with the highest scores would move on to the semi-finals. The top 12 in the semis would then progress to the finals, where the medals would be decided.

Given the setbacks I'd had and the way I'd been diving during training, I was apprehensive in the prelims. Whenever I did a good dive, I was surprised and extremely excited. When I did a below-average dive, I was really disappointed, because I had given a second-rate performance and hadn't presented myself the way I wanted to be seen by the world.

'Don't worry about it,' Chava would reassure me. 'Just keep going.'

Between dives, I would go back into the call room and try to mentally regroup. With so many divers competing, there was a long time to wait, so I had brought my ukulele along. I hid myself away from everyone in a corner of the room behind a partition and strummed very quietly. I like to think it had a more positive effect on me than just sitting there ruminating about how lacklustre my last dive had been.

For the first couple of rounds I was coming 18th or 20th, but by the sixth and final dive, I was in ninth place, which meant I was through to the semi-finals the next morning. I rushed back to the village to have dinner and go to sleep, but it was surprisingly hot in London that night. I kicked off the doona and pressed my whole back up against the cool wall, and I finally managed to fall asleep.

I got up the next day, slammed down two coffees and had my normal breakfast of fruit and yogurt and nuts and seeds. Because there were fewer boys at the pool than the day before, it didn't take as long to warm up and train. I finished about 20 minutes before the end of the session, so Chava and I sat on the pool deck chatting. He's a great person to have around before you compete, because he's so good at reading people. When you need distracting, he does it so naturally and casually that you don't even notice.

In the semis, I maintained the philosophy that Chava had instilled in me and that had worked so well before: to not worry about what the other divers were doing and to relax and enjoy my diving. I was thinking, 'I'm not at my best. But all I can do is try my best'. In the call room everyone watched the competition on television, but at the end of each round when the rankings were about to come on the screen, I walked away and did some stretches. I didn't want to know my ranking in case it affected my thinking or diving. If I was just out of the top 12, I might be tempted to try too hard and then mess up my next dive.

In my first three dives, I did okay. I was more confident before my fourth dive, a reverse three and a half somersault. I knew I could do it well because it was one of the few dives that I had been able to perform consistently during training. I never had any fear about it, because for this dive I use the water to orientate myself, rather than the lights in the ceiling or the height of the platform. The thought running through my head was, 'Yep, this is it. This is going to be awesome'. I walked to the end of the platform, breathed in, breathed out and just went for it. And it felt easy and natural, and when I went through the water I knew I had nailed it.

I even received one of the few 10s awarded in all the diving events at the London Olympics. I wasn't expecting that, and as soon as I looked up at the scoreboard and saw the 10, I threw my hands in the air. When I'm happy and excited, I can't help doing this funny thing where I prance with my knees up really high, as if I'm running into the surf. And that's what I did as I ran over to Chava after that dive. Most divers play it close to their chests during competition, but if I'm happy, I show it (and clap my hands!). I enjoy competing – that's what I do all the training for. I live for it, so when I do a good dive, I really enjoy it and I want people to enjoy it with me.

In the fifth round, I did my arm-stand dive. It wasn't great, and I scored mostly 7.5s from the judges. I like to show my feelings even when I don't do well. I can't fake being the exuberant, happy, boisterous me, but I still acknowledge the crowd and the TV viewers. I wave and look at the camera, because I want to connect with people unconditionally, not just when I've done a good dive. I think that's important because while the Olympics are a competition to see who is faster, higher and stronger, they couldn't really exist without the people who watch it.

My sixth and final dive would be a reprise of my back two and a half somersault with two and a half twists from Beijing. I remember thinking to myself between the fifth and sixth dives that it could be my last 10 metre platform dive in an Olympic competition. That was a good reason to make it a great one, to try and do my best, and to enjoy myself as much as possible. I tried to bring my mind back to the mantra I had used in Beijing: Enjoy the moment. Relax. Have fun.

But even if I got my mind back to its Beijing state, my body felt completely different this time – slow and heavy, less strong and powerful. In 2008, I knew the dive back to front, so I could sense in a split second any slight difference in my body positioning and compensate for it in the next part of the dive. At these Olympics I hadn't had enough preparation time to achieve that same acute spatial awareness and consistency. The dive was different every time I did it – the take-off or twist or entry would vary.

In Beijing, because I was physically stronger and my take-off was more explosive and high, I had enough time at the end of the dive to spot the water and see where I was going to enter. Now I never had enough time, so I had to judge it by feeling alone. During training, I had been going short on the dive so I would hold on to my pike longer.

In the semi-finals, as I took off from the platform I felt underprepared and nervous but also resigned: whatever would be, would be. As I had during training, I held on to my pike – only this time, the dive hadn't actually been going short, so I went over, entering the water with big splash. 'I can't believe I did that,' I thought. 'The one time when the dive wasn't going short.'

When I saw the scores and the rankings, I knew that I hadn't made it into the finals. I was 13th, missing out by one place. I went over to Chava and he gave me a hug. I sat down next to him and watched the rest of the semis, but I don't even remember it because I was crying. I would have liked to have gone out with a bang. I would have liked to have done justice to the rest of my platform career. This was not the way I wanted to be remembered.

I thought of Mum and Lachlan, Greg and Yolande and the kids coming all the way from the other side of the world and now they wouldn't even get to see me compete in the finals. My mind was filled with could haves and should haves: what I could have and should have done differently.

If I had done the arm-stand back two and a half twist that I had taken out of my set since my accidents at the World Cup, that would have given me an extra 30 points or so, which would have taken me up to a respectable score of about 510. But now that I did the maths, even if I had been awarded straight 10s on all of my dives I would have struggled to be in medal contention because the degree of difficulty for my back two and a half somersault with two and a half twists had been downgraded. Everybody in the world has started to use more difficult dives and the DD for those dives has been scaled up to encourage the progression of the sport.

I hadn't performed at the standard I was accustomed to and was known for. I had a reputation for my execution and style and for how beautiful and refined my dives looked. And I wasn't able to bring that to the competition this time. That was what I was most disappointed about, and that's what I had to come to terms with.

There on the pool deck, the work I'd been doing with my psychologist began to kick in. I collected myself and gained some perspective: my performance was purely a product of my preparation, and it had been hampered by everything that had happened in the last couple of years, especially injuries. I had genuinely tried my best. There was nothing else I could have done. It's just the way it happened. I wanted to believe this, and I thought that if I said it enough, then it would start to ring true for me – and it did.

I found solace in the fact that I could not have done more, and in fact I probably should have done *less* in my preparation. I was always rushing, rushing, rushing, trying to do too much, and that's always what got me injured. It sunk in that I had given my all under the circumstances, and this realisation helped me begin to get over the disappointment.

I went back to the village and as I was the first reserve for the finals that evening, I had lunch and took a nap, just in case one of the other boys pulled out. Of course, when I got to the aquatic centre that afternoon, I could see they were all there, so I went out to the pool deck and started taking pictures with Brittany Broben. It was great to be with her, because she was still ecstatic from winning silver in the women's 10 metre platform a couple of days before. She's just the cutest little button: the most excitable little thing, yet so cool and sassy. She is quite mature but she has moments of being a real 16-year-old girl, especially when it comes to Justin Bieber — she goes all weak at the knees. Actually, on my 24th birthday I posted on Facebook and Twitter, 'I'm a twenty-four year old man on the outside (but still a sixteen year old girl on the inside)', so it's no wonder Brittany and I connect so well.

Giaan Rooney came up to me just before the finals started and asked if I would like to do an interview with the Channel 9 commentators, former cricketer and now TV presenter Michael Slater and Michael Murphy, a Commonwealth gold-medal winner in 10 metre platform and 3 metre springboard. She was concerned I might be having a hard time right now so assured me I could decline, but I actually felt fine.

They interviewed me before the competition started, and then we continued chatting as the diving got under way. They involved me in the commentary, asking me questions about the dives. When Tom Daley requested a re-dive during the second round, because he had been distracted by camera flashes from the crowd, they asked me whether or not it was a legitimate concern. Camera flashes had never put me off before, and they were wondering why it hadn't put anybody else off during that round. But all the other competitors had done dives without twists, so they wouldn't have seen the flashes. Doing a dive with a twist, Tom had turned to face the crowd. Also, with Tom being as popular as he is, everyone wanted to get a picture of him diving in the finals.

The commentators kept apologising for keeping me away from the stands and enjoying the rest of the finals, but I saw this as an opportunity to practise my media skills and showcase my abilities outside of diving. I allowed myself to relax and enjoy it. Because I'd never done anything like this before, I didn't pressure myself to be perfect. That showed just how far I'd come in my mental attitude. Before, I would have been so anxious about getting everything right that I probably would have overanalysed everything and jumbled my words. I enjoyed it so much that the time just flew and I was in the box until the end of the fourth round.

I had become so immersed in the spirit of the competition, the excitement and the quality of the diving that I completely forgot about my own disappointment at not being in the final. I had to contain my excitement when I was on air, but as soon as I left the commentary box, I let myself really get into it. Some Mexican girls were using tri-colour body crayons that left a trail on your skin of red, white and green, like the Mexican flag. I used it to put a smiley face on my stomach, and on my back they wrote 'Vamos Pollo', which means 'Let's go, chicken'. Pollo is the nickname of the Mexican boy who was in the final, Ivan Garcia, who ended up placing seventh. They call him that because his dad owns a chicken shop. When his turn came to dive I lifted up my shirt and flashed my back.

After David Boudia from the USA did his last dive, his back two and a half somersault with two and a half twists, I got so excited that I started chanting '10, 10, 10'. Then all the other athletes around me started chanting '10, 10, 10'. The judges didn't listen to us, but David did score an impressive 102.60 for the dive, for an overall score of 568.65, which put him 2 points ahead of Qiu Bo. Tom Daley rounded out the medal winners, taking bronze, to the elation of the Brits in the crowd.

Watching the finals changed my perception of my own gold medal performance in Beijing. I was a different person now compared to the boy whose self-esteem had been so fragile that I'd feared my win was a fluke, that I wasn't the best in the world but just happened to dive the best on the day. Watching as a spectator and seeing how close the competition was between the top divers gave me a new viewpoint. I imagined how the competition must have looked to spectators four years before. I was able to transfer the respect I had for these elite divers in London to myself and my competitors in 2008, and it sunk in that I actually did earn and did deserve my gold medal.

After the final I went and did a big round of media interviews, and when I got back to the village at about 11 that night, David Boudia and Qiu Bo were also just arriving. When I saw David, I started yelling and clapping and ran up to him with my hands in the air. I gave him a big hug. 'Well done, champion, you're my hero,' I said.

He looked completely shell-shocked about his victory – his face bore a deer-in-the-headlights kind of look. I think it was probably how I had looked four years ago, too, because it takes a while for the reality to sink in. Maybe it's because winning a gold medal seems so far outside the realm of possibility. The years and years' worth of dreams and aspirations and fantasies never seem like an actual possibility until it happens. David said to me, 'Now I know how you felt'.

Qiu Bo did an interview with a Chinese newspaper after the Olympics in which he named me as his favourite diver, even though I didn't make it through to the finals. Like all of the Chinese divers, he is very contained during competition, but he can also be the cheekiest, sweetest, most playful boy. I already liked and respected him a lot, so it was really nice to get the feedback that it was mutual.

On the night of the closing ceremony, the atmosphere was amazing as all 10,000 athletes walked from the village over to the stadium. Everyone was on a high from two weeks of Olympic competition. Once we were inside, I hung out with the swimmer Matthew Targett, my good friend basketballer

Liz Cambage, and the Australian volleyball boys, which I'd been doing a lot during the Olympics because I found the height disparity between us quite entertaining. Every time I'd see one particular boy, we'd do a high five. He would hold his hand just above his shoulder and I would have to do a big jump to actually reach it.

It was an incredible night. All that talent in one place, like Annie Lennox, George Michael, Fat Boy Slim and the Spice Girls, plus the light show going on all around the stadium and the costumes and staging – it was the best concert you could go to. There was something happening all the time, something exciting, something cool. I kept thinking, 'Could this evening get any better?' And then it would.

Once the excitement of the closing ceremony was over, I was very much ready to kick into holiday mode. I figured I could do with a rest because I had decided that as soon as I got back to Australia I would go straight into 3 metre springboard training with Chava. I would have been really sad to give up diving completely. I enjoy performing and love the atmosphere and spirit of competition, and shifting to the 3 metre springboard is a way to still have that experience.

From London, Lachlan and I boarded a plane for Rome to visit our friend Jonathan. After three days in the city, Jonathan took us by train to Umbria, near Tuscany, to stay in a villa in the countryside. It was magical. Jonathan's cooking is better than what you can get in any restaurant, and we feasted on ripe tomatoes and juicy peaches, pasta dishes, clams and mussels. There was absolutely nothing to do but lie by the pool and play cards and eat. It was the middle of summer, with scorching 36 to 40 degree days, and first thing in the morning when it was still a bit cool, I'd go down and sunbathe by the pool. There would be a flock of swallows doing figure eights over the water, diving down and dipping in for a drink and somehow never colliding with one another. That was a really nice thing to watch as I sat there soaking up the sunshine and listening to some good Australian chill-out music.

After a week's holiday, I got back to Sydney on a Thursday. By the Monday, I had started training full-on. The last time I had competed in the springboard was only two years before, at the Commonwealth Games in 2010, when I won silver in the 1 metre and in the 3 metre synchro with Ethan Warren. But I have a lot of work to do to catch up with all the progress that 3 metre springboard diving has made since then.

I've got a pretty ambitious set of dives in mind for the Glasgow Commonwealth Games that would put me at the highest degree of difficulty in the world. I started training for these dives straightaway in a new facility where you take off from the springboard and land in a pit filled with big blocks of foam. It's fun playing with dives that maybe a couple of other divers in the world are secretly trying but are certainly not using yet in competition.

It will take a long time to build up the skills I need. I also have a lot of crushing sessions in the gym to look forward to. That's because you have to be able to apply your weight to get power out of the springboard and get enough height and speed as you dive. That's why springboard divers tend to be more heavyset and stronger, especially in the legs, than platform divers. But springboard will be easier on my abs, because it's less ballistic. The movements are much slower and more controlled, so it's going to be gentler on my body overall.

For the first time, I am taking life one day at a time, living in the moment. I can't say for sure what my future will hold, but I do have a dream: to win a gold medal at Glasgow so that I've achieved an Olympic gold, a World Cup gold and a Commonwealth gold – a golden trifecta.

18

growing up

Living in the moment is a very new thing for me. Through all the work I've done with my psychologist, I've come to realise that when I was stressing about the future, it was completely counterproductive. I was worrying about something that wasn't even real, that existed only in my imagination, because no one knows what's coming in the future. The only way I can truly reduce my anxiety is to stay in the present moment and address my thoughts and feelings from here. My life feels richer for doing this, because when I was continually thinking about the future, I was oblivious to my experiences and emotions in the present. It's incredibly liberating to be in training but to not have my whole future planned out. Previously I would have found that incredibly anxiety inducing.

Being more present, I can appreciate how fun diving is. I can appreciate life. I can appreciate Lachlan, who supported my decision to shift my focus to springboard diving because he could see how happy it made me. I can appreciate my mum. We speak every day and live just one suburb away from each other, and she comes with me to training some days just so we can talk during the drive. I appreciate Greg and his family for being so loving and inclusive and unconditionally supportive.

My grandparents are always there for me, too, as they have been since the beginning. My old room in Grandma's house is now my brother Marcus's room, which he stays in when he comes back from boarding school for the holidays. She keeps it set up for him, and there's always a room downstairs for me. Whenever I say I'm coming to Brisbane, Grandma picks me up at the airport and cooks for me and drives me around. She slides right back into that role. I tried to be polite and resist it the first few times but now I just let it happen because I know she likes doing it, and I like her doing it.

I think part of the reason I've been able to let go of worrying about the future is that I have a different perception of myself now, a more stable idea of my worth as a person. I used to think that the only way I would ever feel okay about myself was if I was the best in the world at something – but even after I achieved that I still had the most pitiful self-esteem. I've managed to overcome that type of thinking and I feel good about myself no matter what happens.

This makes all the investment I made on psychology in the year leading up to the London Olympics worth it. I had my doubts. I'm all about doing things that have a tangible outcome; if I can't see it, then it doesn't really exist. But when mental health is your goal, how do you measure it? How do you really know when you've arrived? Because I had no way to gauge my progress, I was worried that I was wasting time and money. I thought that if I didn't win a medal at London I would have even more psychological work to do before I could be okay with myself. If I didn't win, I was afraid that people wouldn't like me any more, that I would be a has-been and that it would affect my job opportunities. I would be a failure in life and would fade to nothingness.

When I did even worse than I had feared at the London Olympics yet was still able to pull myself together, I realised that all the sessions with the psychologist had paid off. I found that I was able to respect and embrace all of my emotions – optimism, elation, joy, nervousness, disappointment, sadness – and to let them show themselves and run their course. And I came out on the other side okay.

I discovered that I still had the love of my family and Lachlan, Chava, my teammates, the media, everyone on Twitter and Facebook. I was amazed by the effort that some people went to, cutting and pasting and Photoshopping inspirational and wonderful messages of support. I finally realised that for people to like me wasn't contingent on just one thing: how well I was diving. This had always been true, but now it had been proven to me, and I'm thankful for that. In the past, I sometimes trawled my Twitter and Facebook pages reading the nice stuff people said about me just to try to bolster my shaky self-esteem. I didn't need to do that any more. I had come to terms with my performance in London and wasn't beating myself up about it, and that meant that I could now appreciate the kind words that people said about me in a more healthy way.

In fact, I feel more empowered and more well liked despite my 'failure'. I'm using quotation marks because I think success and failure are relative. Outward success – a gold medal, being the No.1 men's 10 metre platform diver in the world – hadn't made me a happier person or made my life richer or brought me fulfilment, because I hadn't done the difficult psychological work yet.

My training before Beijing had been entirely physical. I had consciously avoided doing any psychology, as I didn't want to get into all that messy stuff in case it affected me in competition. But because injuries had interrupted my physical training in the lead-up to London, my hardest training was psychological. I developed the mental and emotional maturity to come out of the London Olympics with a better and more positive attitude towards not doing well in competition.

Winning doesn't necessarily mean happiness, and failure can mean growth. When things don't work out in life, it can actually build the strength of your character. And if you celebrate all of your achievements, big and small, you'll always be a winner.

The mental training I did was really uncomfortable, but the reward is that I am a happier, more positive and more mature person. My hard work, physical and mental, has reaped almost everything I have ever dreamed of. All I ever wanted was an Olympic gold medal and to be happy, healthy and wealthy. Well, I'm not wealthy yet, but I'm happy and healthy.

The success I've had in my diving career and the gains I've made psychologically are both lifelong achievements. I'm always going to be an Olympic champion, and I'm always going to be able to draw upon the mental and emotional resilience I've developed.

I think I can be a better role model now that I can connect with a wider range of my emotions. Expressing happiness and love came freely and naturally to me, but I tried to suppress the 'bad' emotions. I used to do everything I could to bury emotions such as anger, sadness, shame and guilt. That's what did the most damage to me, because those emotions came out sideways. I have been learning how to express those feelings so that they don't compound and snowball inside me.

I especially had a fear about feeling or showing anger, because of the way Mum used to yell at me and hit me when I was a kid. I'm still learning the boundaries of anger and how to express it appropriately. But I'm not reaching for the pillbox and I'm not smashing up cheap razors to get the blades out to cut myself in the shower when I'm angry at someone.

You can't put a price on self-worth and self-esteem and mental health. You can try and shut off your mind – that's what I tried to do with drugs – but it doesn't work. Little did I know that trying to block out troubling thoughts and feelings only exacerbates the problem. You have to face all this stuff eventually, so it's much better to face it head on. Dealing with painful feelings and memories is really hard work at the beginning. It might mean looking at awful stuff, and the results don't come straightaway. It's like training for the Olympics: you can't rush it, and it takes practice. But the benefit is so worthwhile.

Many people underestimate the need to treat mental health problems, because you can't see, hear or touch them. But feelings are just as real and powerful as any physical illness. No matter how painful or uncomfortable those feelings are, though, they are not insurmountable – so long as you get help.

I tried to do it alone. I thought it was a sign of weakness to talk about my feelings. I thought that to be masculine meant not expressing emotions. And I was ashamed, because I felt I had no good reason to feel the way I felt.

Now I know that no one should ever feel that they need to have a reason for being depressed. Some depression arises from trauma. Some people are physiologically predisposed to depression and can be equally depressed even when the world is at their feet.

Because of the shame I felt, I never wanted to discuss it with my sports psychologist. And that's why my depression and anxiety lasted for so many years.

I can't stress enough the benefit of reaching out. A problem shared is a problem halved. If I had known then that you can't do it by yourself and that it is actually a sign of strength to ask for help, I would have done it. As a teenager I thought I knew everything, and apparently I didn't.

Actually, the older I get, the more I realise how much I still have to learn and experience and do. This is only the first chapter of my life, but if the first 24 years are anything to go by, I'm really looking forward to seeing how the rest of the story goes ...

Thank you ...

Lachlan: for being there through thick and thin, and teaching me so much.

Mum: for getting knocked up by Matt Mitcham's dad, and plenty of good memories.

Grandma: for being a reliable constant throughout my life, and not once giving me the impression that I was a burden.

Grandad: for always being the silent supporter.

Cath: I don't even want to think about how different the last six years would have been without your support.

New South Wales Institute of Sport – particularly Charles Turner: for taking a chance with me, for fighting bureaucratic battles for me, and your care for my welfare as a human being before an athlete.

Diving Australia: I am amazed and humbled by how the relationship has changed in recent years, and I genuinely feel valued and supported by DA, and hope to continue our relationship for a long time to come.

Australian Institute of Sport, NSW Diving, Australian Olympic Committee, Australian Sports Commission, Australian Commonwealth Games Association, Alan, Queensland Diving Association, and the Australian Government (for years of support and social security).

My sponsors Funky Trunks, Foxtel and Telstra. And also thanks to CAA, Hot Tuna, Coles and Promax Nutrition for their support.

A special thanks to John and John, as well as Johnson & Johnson

Sarina and the Orion crew

SPP, Brian, Marc, Craig & Dr Chen during the tough times.

The University of Sydney

The Sports Group

Larry Writer

Fiona, Vanessa, and Rachel and HarperCollins

Family, friends and fans

Mitchams, Smiths, Fletchers, Coutts', Harradines, Tylers, Blackshaws, Linnells, Whetstones, Bevis', Willacys, Di Cellos, Nicolls, Dixons and my 'second family', the Williams', whose love and generosity made me feel part of the family during a time in my life when I needed it most.

Lastly, the way in which the Swadlings embraced me, automatically making me part of their family was … to be honest, unsettling at first. How could this seemingly traditional, grounded, functional, wholesome, stable family care so much for a stranger who could be as deranged as Hannibal Lecter or Emily Rose? And yet they did.

If you haven't been mentioned here, then you can assume that you are the most valued of them all as I always inevitably forget to thank the most important person. Just as I nearly forgot to thank Chava (again!) …

THANK YOU.

Picture credits

Page 7: Photos courtesy of Matthew Mitcham
Page 8 top left: Courtesy of Alexis Paszek
Page 8 top right and bottom: Photos by John McRae, ©johnmcrae
Page 9 top: 'Cross' by Maree Azzopardi, © Maree Azzorpardi
Page 9 bottom: 'Metamorphic Matt' by Renato Grome, © Renato Grome
Page 10: Photo by John McRae, ©johnmcrae
Page 11: Photo by Julie Adams for *marie claire* magazine Australia, courtesy of
  marie claire
Page 12 top: Courtesy of Matthew Mitcham
Page 12 bottom: Courtesy of Rod Smith
Page 13: Photos courtesy of Matthew Mitcham
Page 14 top right and left: Photos courtesy of Matthew Mitcham
Page 14 bottom: Photo by John McRae, ©johnmcrae courtesy of Ausin Tung
  Gallery
Page 15: Photos courtesy of Matthew Mitcham
Page 16: Photo by Terry Trewin, courtesy of Funky Trunks

Picture Section 3:
Page 1 top: Photo by Rachel Bugg, courtesy of Matthew Mitcham
Page 1 bottom: Photo by Jaele Patrick, courtesy of Matthew Mitcham
Pages 2–3: Photos courtesy of Matthew Mitcham
Page 4 top: Courtesy of Rachel Bugg
Page 4 middle: Courtesy of Matthew Mitcham
Page 4 bottom: Courtesy of Rachel Bugg
Page 5: Photos courtesy of Matthew Mitcham
Page 6 top: Courtesy of Annabelle Smith
Page 6 middle and bottom: Courtesy of Matthew Mitcham
Page 7: Photos courtesy of Matthew Mitcham
Pages 8–9: Photos courtesy of Matthew Mitcham
Page 10 top: Courtesy of Matthew Mitcham
Page 10 bottom: Courtesy of Tom Daley
Page 11 top: Courtesy of Wesley Sabugo
Page 11 bottom: Courtesy of Matthew Mitcham
Page 12–13: Photos courtesy of Matthew Mitcham
Page 13 top: Courtesy of Matthew Mitcham
Page 14 top: 'Photographing Matthew Mitcham # 4' by William Yang,
  © William Yang
Page 14 bottom: 'The Adventures of Droplet the Elf' by Francesca Martí,
  © Francesca Martí
Page 15: Photos courtesy of Matthew Mitcham
Page 16 top: Courtesy of Ian Carlos Gonçalves de Matos
Page 16 bottom: Photo by John McRae, ©johnmcrae courtesy of Ausin Tung
  Gallery

About the author

Matthew Mitcham performed the single greatest dive in Olympic history at the 2008 Beijing Olympics, scoring perfect 10s, and won gold for Australia.

Born in Brisbane in 1988, Matthew was already a champion trampoline gymnast at 11 when he was discovered by the Australian Institute of Sport Diving Program and joined the Talent Identification Squad.

In 2005 he won his first of many national titles and the following year represented Australia at the Commonwealth Games. After taking a break in 2006, he returned in 2007 to train under his present coach, Chava Sobrino, at the NSW Institute of Sport.

After his historic gold medal win at Beijing on the 10 metre platform, he won *The Age* and *Sydney Morning Herald*'s 2008 Australian Sports Performer of the Year Award. He was also joint winner, with pole vaulter Steve Hooker, of the Sports Australia Hall of Fame's 2008 Don Award, named after Sir Donald Bradman, 'for the athlete who most inspired the nation' and upheld Sir Donald's traits of 'sportsmanship, courage, dignity, integrity and modesty'.

He went on to win gold at both the FINA World Cup and the Canada Cup in 2010, finishing the year ranked No.1 in the world in the 10 metre platform. At the 2010 Commonwealth Games he won four silver medals. Struggling with injury in 2011, he won gold at the Canada Cup but a torn abdominal muscle forced him to withdraw from further competition in 2011.

A star attraction at the London Olympics, Matthew's popularity at home and abroad soared. Despite not winning a medal and having a smaller fan-base than his more famous teammates, he was the most influential Australian Olympian on Twitter. He scored the highest influence score of 83.8 in Edelman Public Relations' TweetLevel program, which analyses popularity, engagement and trust.

On his return from the Olympics he was named one of Australia's Top 10 most influential people under 30 on social media. On Facebook alone he has a devoted band of more than 80,000 fans from Australia, the US, Italy, Mexico, Canada and China, and more than 40,000 Twitter followers.

Joyously out and proud, Matthew is a role model for his courage in and out of the pool. He has consistently featured in the Top 25 list of most influential gay Australians from 2008 to 2012.

Matthew is an Australian Men's Health Ambassador and Youth Ambassador for the Pacific Friends of the Global Fund.

He is also in demand as a motivational public speaker, from talking to young people about being the best they can be to addressing corporations about the importance of pro-diversity in the workplace.

Matthew is back training full time with coach Chava Sobrino at the NSW Institute of Sport, this time for world domination on the 3 metre springboard.